Cybertheology

Cybertheology

THINKING CHRISTIANITY IN THE ERA
OF THE INTERNET

ANTONIO SPADARO

Translated by Maria Way

FORDHAM UNIVERSITY PRESS

New York   2014

Cybertheology: Thinking Christianity in the Era of the Internet
was first published in Italian as *Cyberteologia. Pensare il
cristianesimo al tempo della rete*, © Vita e Pensiero, 2012.

Fordham University Press has no responsibility for the
persistence or accuracy of URLs for external or third-party
Internet websites referred to in this publication and does not
guarantee that any content on such websites is, or will
remain, accurate or appropriate.

Fordham University Press also publishes its books in a
variety of electronic formats. Some content that appears in
print may not be available in electronic books.

Library of Congress Control Number: 2014938461

Printed in the United States of America

16 15 14   5 4 3 2 1

First edition

Contents

Preface

Is the Internet Changing the Way You Think? This is the title of a 2011 collection of interviews, edited by John Brockman, on the impact of the Internet on our lives. Is the Internet changing our way of thinking? The recent digital technologies are no longer tools or devices that exist totally apart from our bodies and minds. The Internet is not an instrument; it is an *ambience* which surrounds us. The handheld devices that permit us to be connected at all times are becoming ever lighter and smaller, making life's digital dimensions almost transparent. They are open doors that are rarely closed. Who turns off an iPhone anymore? One charges it and puts it on vibrate, but one rarely turns it off. There are some who do not even know how to turn one off. If one carries a smartphone in one's pocket, then one is always connected to the Internet.

Not surprisingly, a growing number of studies looks at the ways in which the Internet is changing our everyday lives and, more generally, our relationships with the world and with the people who are close to us. However, if the Internet is changing our ways of living and thinking, does it not also change (and thus is already changing) our way of thinking about and living the faith?

I've been asking myself this question since January 2010, when I received an invitation to give a talk at a conference entitled "Digital Witnesses." The invitation came from Monsignor Domenico Pompili, the director of the Office for Social Communications at the Italian Bishops' Conference. The director had asked me to talk about faith and the Internet. Since 1999, I have written many articles on individual aspects of the Internet and on single networks in *La Civiltà Cattolica*. My talk in some ways was an extension of my work for the journal and its strong propositions. I became its director in October 2011. The journal's interests in communication started with Father Enrico Baragli, a real pioneer in studies of the mass media, who was followed by Father Antonio Stefanizzi, who wrote articles on new communication technologies. When I received Monsignor Pompili's invitation, I had already published *Nuove forme della cultura al tempo di internet* (*New Forms of Culture in the Era of the Internet*) (2006), and *Reti di relazione* (*Nets of Relationships*) (2010). However, that invitation put me at a disadvantage. I understood that they were not asking for an exploration of a phenomenology of the instruments of the Internet that could be used for evangelization. I was asked to present a sociological reflection on religiosity on the Internet but simple reflections alone did not seem to be sufficient to me. I remember that, when I tried to organize my speech, I stared at a blank computer screen with no idea about where to begin or what to write. I understood that I needed to give a theological speech. It was the moment to say something that was perhaps the fruit of the cognitive impulse that faith frees from oneself in a time like our own, when the Internet's logic shows us ways of thinking, knowing, communicating, and living. I had started to explore a territory that, to me, still seemed to be rather untouched. Bibliographical research helped me understand that a lot had already been written on the pastoral dimension, which understood the Internet as an instrument of evangelization. What, it appeared to me, was less well studied was a systematic and theological reflection on the topic. My questions were: What impact has the Internet had on the ways in which we understand the Church and ecclesial communion? What impact has it had on the ways in which we think about Revelation, grace, the liturgy, the sacraments, and the classic themes of theology? My April 23, 2010, lecture at the "Digital Witnesses" conference was the first step toward a personal reflection that I still consider to be in its initial phase. The need to confront these questions with courage began to be shared. On February 28, 2011, Benedict XVI, addressing participants at the Plenary Session of the Pontifical Council for Social Communication, said:

> It is not just that we need to explain the message of the Gospel in today's language, but we have to have the courage to think in a way that is more profound, as happened at other times, about the relationship between the faith, the life of the Church, and the changes that man is living. The task of helping those who have responsibility in the Church to be able to understand, interpret, and talk this "new language" of the media in pastoral situations (cf. *Aetatis novae*, 2) and in dialogue with the contemporary world, asking: What are the challenges that the so-called "digital thought" puts on the faith and on theology? What questions are needed? The world of communication interests the whole of the cultural universe, social and spiritual, of the human being. If the new languages have an impact on the way we think and live, this is in some way relevant also to the world of the faith, its intelligence and its expression. Theology, according to a classic definition, is the intelligence of the faith, and we know well that intelligence, understood as reflective and critical knowledge, is not extraneous to the cultural changes that are underway. Digital culture puts new tasks on our ability to speak and to listen to a symbolic language that speaks of the transcendent. Jesus himself, in his proclamation of the Kingdom of God, knew how to use elements of the culture and ambience of his time: the flocks, the fields, the banquet, seeds, and so on. Today we are called to discover, in digital culture also, the symbols and metaphors that are significant to the people and that can be helpful in speaking about the Kingdom of God to contemporary man. (Benedict XVI 2011a)

This book is my first attempt to answer that call, and it already has an ample and ecumenical life. In any case, thinking about faith in the era of the Internet is not only a reflection in the faith's service; it is both higher and more global. If Christians reflect on the Internet, it is not only in regard to learning how to "use" it, but as an environment to "inhabit." As John Paul II wrote in his Apostolic Letter of January 24, 2005, "The Rapid Development": "The Church, which in light of the message of salvation entrusted to it by the Lord is also a teacher of humanity, recognizes the duty to offer its own contribution for a better understanding of outlooks and responsibilities connected with current developments in communications" (John Paul II, 2005). This is the Church's major contribution to the Web, at least from her own viewpoint: to help humans to better understand the profound significance of communication and the media, above all because they "influence the consciousness of individuals, they form the mentality and determine their vision of things" (ibid.). In the development of communication, the Church sees the actions of God, who moves humanity toward a completion. The Internet is, at least in its power, a space of communion that is part of our journey toward this completion. In Christ, we must therefore have a spiritual look at the Web, seeing Christ who calls humanity to be ever more unified and connected.

Another word of warning is in order: I am neither a sociologist nor a computer scientist. On the basis of my academic training—first in philosophy and then in theology—my reflections on the Internet are derived from literary criticism, which has shaped my views since 1994, and my involvement with *Civiltà Cattolica*. It was the critical reading of poetry that led me to become involved with technology, and only theology was able to provide me with the right amount of curiosity and the right categories through which to understand the Internet. The experience of Marshall McLuhan, who faced the new media with an innovative way of looking at them both from a critical literary viewpoint and as a Catholic thinker, has been a comfort and inspiration to me. The poet Gerard Manley Hopkins helped me understand the role of technological innovation; jazz helped me understand the role of social networks; and the theologians—from Thomas Aquinas to Teilhard de Chardin—shed light on the forces that drive us in the world, participating in Creation, and that lift us toward a goal that exceeds it, well beyond any cognitive surplus. It is the research into deeper meanings that allowed me to understand the value of the USB cable that I have in my hand. I know that my iPad has nothing to do with my unquenchable desire to know the world, while my Galaxy Note tells me (even when it is on silent) that I am not meant to remain alone. T. S. Eliot helped me understand how to avoid his own pitfalls. However, Flannery O'Connor helped me understand the importance of the "action of grace in territory held largely by the devil." I thus understand that, if I also see a lot of evil on the Web, I cannot dwell on negative judgment alone if I want to see God in the world's work. And when I see electricity invading my computer, turning it on and making it perform prodigiously, it is the poetry of Karol Wojtyla which tried to explain electrical metaphors used in the Sacrament of Confirmation that draws my astonishment.

Technology, then, explains our desire for a fullness that we always supersede, whether at the level of presence and relationships, or at the level of knowledge: cyberspace underlines our finitude and draws us to satiety. To see it, in some way signifies operating in a field in which spirituality and technology intersect.

Obviously, the pages that follow should be considered as an introduction to a work that is, and will always be, in progress. Since April 23, 2010, I have written a series of articles in *La Civiltà Cattolica* that have led me to engage my reflections at various conferences and meetings, both in Italy and abroad (for example, in Brazil, where that country's Bishops' Council organized a seminar for the bishops that was dedicated to communication on the Web). If my reflection continues, it is also thanks to the wise stimulus of the Pontifical Council for Social Communication, above all in the person of Monsignor Claudio Celli, and the intellectual encouragement of the Pontifical Council for Culture, above all in the person of Cardinal Gianfranco Ravasi. It has been a great honor to be named as a consulter to these two Vatican dicasteries. Even though a fundamental part of my reflections on *cybertheology* has been refuted in some writings in *La Civiltà Cattolica*, I have felt a need to provide them for comparison and debate on the Internet. This is why on January 1, 2011, I started my blog, Cyberteologia.it, and then my Facebook page, Cybertheology, a Twitter account (@antoniospadaro), and "The CyberTheology Daily" (http://www.cyber-theology.net), which is a content curation service, as well as a series of other initiatives. In these ways I have sought to render my reflections "social." Finally, since April 2011, I have been editing a column on cybertheology in the monthly magazine *Jesus*.

Consequently, this book is part of an ecosystem of reflections that has developed at many colloquia and through exchanges of ideas with friends and scholars who have helped me to live this research as the fruit of a profound and ample sharing, and for this input I am sincerely grateful.

It is my hope that readers of this book will pick up some elements that form a type of conceptual premise. Firstly, I want to reiterate that the correct questions with which to start to read this book relate to the new existential context that is generated by the media, and to the "anthropological mutation" that results: What is its significance for the faith? In which world do we live? Is it the same one that it used to be? What is the answer to "where do we live?" Today, we also inhabit a digital space. In the digital era, we adopt values that are affected by the fact that the "Word was made flesh and came amongst us."

To me, then, it is important to remember that this book's intent is to unveil scenarios and to feed the desire; not to halt at the "wonders" of technology, but to go to its basis so as to understand how the world is changing and how this change is having an impact on the life of faith. The technologies are new, not simply because they are different from those that preceded them but because they profoundly change the very concept of having an experience. The ingenuity to believe that they will be at our disposal means neglecting the modification of anything in the way we perceive reality. The Church's duty, like that of all the individual ecclesial communities, is to accompany us on our journey, and the Web has become an integral and irreversible part of this path.

August 6, 2011

Cybertheology

CHAPTER I

The Internet
Between Theology and Technology

Some eighty years after the first commercial use of steam loco-motives, Thomas Hardy's novel *Jude the Obscure* (1895) was published. In those pages, Sue Bridehead rebuffs Jude's sugges-tion that they sit together in the cathedral: "Cathedral? Yes. Though I think I'd rather sit in the railway station. . . . That's the centre of the town life now." In this exchange, the station is not a *nonspace*, a place of speedy transit; it becomes the center of connections in the heart of the city. The station has become an environment that is also symbolic and not just a simple de-pot for a means of transport. If this is true of the railway sta-tion, it is even more so of the Internet (and by extension the Web) today.

The historian Harold Perkin wrote that the men who built the railway were not only creating a means of transport but also contributing to the creation of a new society and of a new world (Perkin 1970). Those who lived through the rise of the railway in the middle of the nineteenth century considered this means of transport not merely as something new but revolutionary—the railway revolution,[1] a cultural metaphor at the time. It is interesting to note that every invention that has permitted us to expand and intensify communication and exchange networks—from the printing press to the railway to the telegraph and now the Internet—has been considered revolutionary. If labeling progress *revolutionary* helps us to understand the social relevance of innovations, it also risks hiding a consideration that is more important: innovations seem to respond to our age-old desires for relationships, communication, and knowledge. Seen in this light, the invention of the Internet is perhaps less a novelty of our time than an extension of our desire for communal life and knowledge.

THE INTERNET AND EVERYDAY LIFE

Technology always seems to bring with it an aura that provokes astonishment and disquiet. What are the motives that lie behind and generate these feelings? Is it because technology appears to be able to realize something that responds to our ancient desires and profound fears? Is that why technological innovations touch us, intimidate us, and make us wonder? The Internet is a reality that is part of the everyday lives of many people. We can no longer simply ignore the Internet and return to an "innocent" time, since the functioning of our "primary" world, of the means of communication of every type, is based on the existence of this so-called virtual world that surrounds us (Ottmar 2005; Granieri 2009). Today, the Internet is a place that we frequent in order to stay in contact with friends who live far away, to read the news, to buy a book, to book a vacation, or to share interests and ideas: "It is a space for humans, a space that is populated by human beings. It no longer has a context that is anonymous and aseptic, but has a scope that is anthropologically qualified" (Pompili 2011, 62).

The Internet is a space for experience that is becoming an integral part of everyday life, in a fluid way: a "new existential context."[2] The Internet is therefore not at all a simple *instru-*

ment of communication, which one can choose to use, but it has evolved into a cultural "environment" (Ellul 1980) that determines a style of thought, creating new territories and new types of education, contributing also to the definition of a new way to stimulate the intelligence and to tighten relationships. It is a way to live in and organize our world (Spadaro 2006; Giaccardi 2010). It is not a separate environment, but it is becoming ever more integrated into our everyday lives. As a result, it is not a specific place that we enter at any given time so we can "live" online for a while and then to return to our offline lives.

One of the major challenges—especially for those who are not so-called digital natives—is to dismiss the Internet as a parallel reality (that is, one that is separate from our everyday lives) rather than seeing it as an anthropological space that is deeply intertwined with our everyday lives. Instead of making us leave our world to delve into the virtual world, technology has made the digital world penetrate our ordinary world. The digital media are not doors through which we escape from our reality; they are extensions that enrich our capacity to live out relationships and to exchange information.

THE LIGHTNESS OF DEVICES

The Internet (and by extension the Web) is becoming ever more transparent and invisible. It has an exponential tendency to be no longer the other of our everyday lives. We know very well that to be "wired" or connected, we no longer need to sit in front of a computer; all we need is a smartphone in our pockets,[3] perhaps with push notifications enabled.[4] The Internet is a plane of existence that is becoming more and more integrated with the other planes of our human existence; we no longer perceive the digital media surrounding us as separate entities— they seem to melt into our environment to the point where we hardly notice them anymore (Pompili 2011, 66–68). Think, for example, of tablets like the iPad or its competitors. Like our cell phones, they are always already turned on, and the time it takes for individual applications to open is negligible, as is switching from one application to another. Nothing now exists that separates us from a screen; everything can be done at the touch of a finger. Even when we want to type some text, we can do so with the help of an on-screen keyboard. It is only on a superficial level that these characteristics seem to be unimportant. In reality, they are radically changing the way we interact with a technological device and use this digital resource. Our relationship with touchscreens becomes physical and our fingers seem to reach (virtually) "inside" the screen. Furthermore, these actions are performed on a small handheld device that only weighs around 1.4 pounds (or less) and can be used anywhere, unlike a desktop computer. Touchscreen technology has become a part of our everyday lives, from automated teller machines to self check-in kiosks at the airport to self check-out machines at the supermarket. The iPad take this type of relationship to digital content to a whole new level, and the barriers between users and product tend to vanish into thin air. In this way, the device is becoming a window, an open frame onto the world of the Web.

If we consider the ease of use of the iPad or similar tablets and their applications, we can see the device is beginning to lose its technological aura, leaving space for a relationship that is more immediate and direct, without any visible mediation. The obstacles to how we interact with a computer—the power-up time, mouse, keyboard, and portability—have been reduced significantly. We are no longer looking at a machine with a liquid crystal display or iron particles on a rigid hard disk. The device becomes, in some way, transparent to the person who has it in his or her hands.

Think about what we are able to accomplish thanks to a device as lightweight and portable as the iPad, the iPhone, or an Android smartphone: We can participate in events and conferences while we are sitting at our desks or traveling the world. We can speak with people who live in another part of the world.

We can perform transactions and order goods on the go, and more. There is an evident displacement that causes the borders between the body and technological devices to become less defined.

A RE-FORMATION OF THE MIND

Human beings do not remain unchanged when the world around them changes: it is not only the means of communication that are transformed, but the self and its culture. Throughout history, technological advances have transformed the lives and sense of self of human beings. In synthesis, they make up what is almost a story of the human experience of technology. Pierre Lévy, who famously studied the cultural implications of informatization, wrote: "It is the same man who speaks, buries his own dead and naps flints, spreading to us Prometheus' fire to cook our food, to dry the clay, to work with metal, to feed the steam engines, to run along the high voltage cables, to burn in nuclear power plants, to release himself from the arms of war and from the instruments of destruction" (Lévy 2001, 3). He asks rhetorically: "Do technologies come perhaps from another planet, the world of cold machines with no emotions, without any significance or human value, as a certain tradition of thought tends to suggest?" His answer is clear:

> It seems to me, on the contrary, that it is not only technologies that are imagined, realized and re-interpreted when they are used by men, but that it is rather their own intensive use of tools that constitutes humanity as such, or, better, that contributes in a determinate manner to his constitution as we know it. To give an expression that synthesises this: "the human world is, by definition technological." (Ibid.)

It is thus that our humanity unfolds, through the architecture that protects and welcomes us; through the routes and navigation systems that open up new horizons to us; through writing, the telephone, and the cinema, which we fill with signs and

symbols. Think of the invention of the alphabet and its importance for our progress toward civil institutions, for example; we
can be citizens of a complex world because we can write (and
read) the laws. Our world would look very different without
the invention of fire, the wheel, and the alphabet. Human beings have always sought to interpret the world through technologies that have allowed us to capture a semblance of the
world around us, such as photography and motion pictures,
for example; representations that open new cognitive spaces
for interaction between the subject and the outside world.
Technology is, therefore, not an ensemble of modern "*avant-garde*
objects" (Turkle 2008). Through use of these means human
beings exercise their own capacity for knowledge, freedom,
and responsibility.[5]

The Internet is, therefore, a reality that is necessarily becoming ever more interesting to a believer, affecting his or her capacity to comprehend reality and therefore his or her faith and
way of living it. One's faith and the way of living it are influential in their interventions into a person's experiences, permitting
him or her to increase his or her human potential. The influence
they exert, with which we are more or less conversant, depends
in good measure on our perception of ourselves, of others, and
of the world. Without prejudices, they can be considered to be
resources, even though they require critical scrutiny and wise
and responsible usage (CEI 2010, no. 51).

It is evident that the Internet, emerging from a long history
of innovations and technological advances, cannot but have an
effect on the comprehension of the faith and the Church. The
logic of the Internet can model theological logic, and the Internet now poses interesting challenges for the comprehension of
Christianity itself, highlighting both what is compatible and the
possible incompatibilities. *Redemptoris Missio* (no. 37)—published
in 1990, a year after the Web's invention and some three years
before it began to reach a larger public—states that the media
have not only the channels to spread the news and gossip many
times over but that there is also a more profound reason why

the evangelization of modern culture to a great degree depends on their influence. It is not enough to use the media to spread the Christian message and the Magisterium of the Church; there is a need to integrate the message itself into this new culture that has been created by modern communication. This is a complex problem because that culture was born before the creation of its content since there are new ways of communicating, with new languages, new techniques, and new psychological attitudes. John Paul II understood well that a re-formation of the mind was necessary (Tremolada 2009).

Fundamentally, Christianity is a communicative event. Everything in Christian Revelation and the pages of the Bible exudes communication: the heavens tell us about the glory of God, angels are his messengers, and the prophets speak in his name. The Bible, in its own way—with its interpretations of angels, the burning bush, tablets of stone, dreams, donkeys, whispers and breaths of light wind—becomes one of the media that realize this communication. And the Christian news has, in Christ's invitation to "go into the whole world and proclaim the gospel to every creature" (Mark 16.15), which is its thrust. On the other hand, the words of Exodus 20.4 are precise: "You shall not carve idols for yourselves in the shape of anything in the sky above or on the earth below or in the waters beneath the earth."[6] The God of Exodus puts us on our guard against making images, from a technology that substantially exposes idolatry and reduces the other to something amongst other things. These two Bible verses, in essence, describe well the constant dialectic of Christians on the Web and their approach to the technology of communication: news that is based on knowledge and relationships is one thing, the technology that models its own media idols is quite another.

The Church is naturally present where humans develop their capacity for knowledge and relationships. Announcing a message and relationships of communion have always been two of the founding pillars of her being. The task, therefore, does not have to be how to *use* the Web well, as is often thought, but how to *live well* in the era of the Web. In this sense, the Web is not a new *means* of evangelization but is, above all, a context in which the faith is called to express itself not by a mere willingness to be present, but by the compatibility of Christianity with the lives of human beings.[7]

THE SPIRITUALITY OF TECHNOLOGY

Technology is not only, as the most skeptical believe, a means to live the illusion of taming the forces of nature so as to lead a happy life. It would be reductive to consider this only as the fruit of a will for power and domination. It is rather "a profoundly human fact, tied to the autonomy and liberty of man" (Benedict XVI 2009a, no. 69). Through technology, "the mastery of the spirit over the material" is expressed and confirmed, and at the same time human aspirations and the tensions of our soul are manifested. Technology is, therefore, the organizational force exercised on the material by a knowing human project. In this sense, technology is ambiguous, because our freedom also can be used for evil (no. 70). It is just because of our nature that technology makes its mark on our way of understanding the world and not just on our way of living it:

> It is impossible to separate the human being from his material environment, from the signs and images through which he makes sense of life and the world. In the same way, one cannot separate the material world—and even less its artificial part—from the ideas through which technological objects are conceived and used by the men who invent them, produce them and use them. (Lévy 2001, 4)

For example, the airplane has led us to understand the world in a way that is different from the way we understood it after the invention of the wheeled cart; likewise, the printing press has made us understand culture in a different way. However, it is also true that both the airplane and the printing press have made us understand human beings better. The believer knows how to see the human response to the call of God, to which we give shape and transform creation, and thus even himself, through technology with the help of devices and procedures (Monsma 1986). In that same sense, John Paul II (2013) called for a "sacralisation" of human ingenuity. Benedict XVI (2009, nos. 70, 77), in his turn, spoke of the "extraordinary potential of the new technologies," which he defined as "a true gift to humanity." A question arises spontaneously at this point: if technology, in particular the digital revolution, changes our way of thinking, then does this not mean that we, in some way have to reconsider the faith and how to communicate it (Benedict XVI 2011).[8]

A crucial moment in the spiritual understanding of the new technologies was the promulgation of the Decree of the Second Vatican Council, *Inter Mirifica,* on December 4, 1963, which exhorts:

> Among the wonderful technological discoveries which men of talent, especially in the present era, have made with God's help, the Church welcomes and promotes with special interest those which have a most direct relation to men's minds and which have uncovered new avenues of communicating most readily news, views and teachings of every sort. The most important of these inventions are those media which, such as the press, movies, radio, television and the like, can, of their very nature, reach and influence, not only individuals, but the very masses and the whole of human society, and thus can rightly be called the media of social communication. (No. 1)

In June 19, 1964, Paul VI, visiting the Automation Center at the Aloisianum of Gallarate, used words that, in my opinion, are of a disconcerting beauty. The center was working on an electronic analysis of the *Summa Theologicae* of St. Thomas Aquinas, and also on the text of the Bible.

> Science and technology, once more twinned, are prodigious and, at the same time, have let us glimpse new mysteries. However, it is enough for Us to grasp the inner meaning of this Audience, to note that in the modern context, this service is at the disposal of culture; as the mechanical brain comes to the aid of the spiritual one, and

how much more is expressed in its own language, that is, thought, which seems to like to be dependent on it. Have you not begun to apply coded procedures to the text of the Latin Bible? What will happen? Is it, perhaps, that this sacrosanct text will be reduced to marvellous games by the mechanics of automation, like any other insignificant text? Or, is it not this effort of infusing into mechanical instruments the reflection of spiritual functions, which is ennobled and raised to become a service that touches the sacred? Is it the spirit that has become imprisoned by the material, or is it perhaps that the material, already given and required to execute the laws of the spirit, offers to the spirit itself a sublime respect? It is at this point that Our Christian ear can hear the groaning of which Saint Paul speaks (Romans, 8, 22), the groaning of natural creatures who aspire to a higher level of spirituality?[9]

Paul VI affirms that the "mechanical brain comes to the aid of the spiritual one." He adds that man makes the "effort to infuse the mechanical instruments with the reflection of spiritual functions" and continues by affirming that, thanks to technology, the material offers "to the same spirit, a sublime respect." The pope hears the cries of an aspiration for a higher level of spirituality that are rising from *homo tecnologicus*. The technological being is still a spiritual being.[10]

Technological development can "induce the idea of the self-sufficiency of the technology itself when man asks himself only 'how?,' and does not consider the many, because from them he is pushed to act"; the absolutism of technique "tends to produce an incapacity to perceive that which cannot be explained simply by the material" (Benedict XVI 2009a, nos. 70, 77). If this has been understood correctly, it can instead be expressed as a form of longing for "transcendence" in regard to the human condition (see George 2006, 87–90; Beaudoin 1998, 87), so that it is lived currently. One must also say this of that "open space of communication for intercommunication in the world by computers and informatic memories," that is, so-called cyberspace.[11] The theologian Tom Beaudoin has noted that this space—so unusual because of the rapidity of its connections—represents the desire of human beings for a fullness that is always at a higher level, whether of presence and relationships or of knowledge. "Cyberspace underlines our finitude," "reflects our desire for the infinite, the divine." Seeking such fullness signifies, then, working in a field "in which spirituality and technology intersect" (Beaudoin 1998, 87).[12]

This alone is certainly not a topic that is relevant to today only. It was amenable, for example, to reflection by Cardinal Avery Dulles, who, at the start of the 1970s, proposed to uncover in this way "the changing styles of communication that are influencing the knowledge of the Church, in its nature, in its message, in its mission" (Dulles 1971, 5),[13] insisting on the relationships between theology and communication. One can continue on the dense network of reports that this interest has developed across time (Soukup, 1983).[14] Recent research has found at least seven areas for reflection:

Pastoral theology, which relates to the communication of the Christian message.

Applied theology, which uses its own theological instruments to respond to the demands of communication.

The application of theological categories (the Trinity, incarnation, etc.) to communication, so as to be able to understand them better.

The use of instruments of communication to analyze religious texts.

The use of the content of film, television, music, and so on to promote theological reflection.

The study of communication as a context for theology.

The use of the structures of communication to modulate theological reflection.

In this present context, it is the last two areas of reflection that are of interest. By pausing at these intersections, one obtains a desire to verify the possibility of a "cybertheology." Even if experiences that are specifically religious cannot be understood as being dependent on communication techniques, it is evident that telematic technologies are beginning to have an influence on the way we think the Christian faith and, above all, on the categories of comprehension. Obviously, I do not intend to put forward some sort of technological determinism but, rather, to propose a reflection on the context in which it is already developing today, and on the ways in which theological reflection will develop tomorrow.

INFORMATICS, LANGUAGE, AND THE INTELLIGENCE OF THE FAITH

If we want to see how telematic technologies are beginning to influence the way of thinking the Christian faith and its language we have to look no further than the field of informatics and its use of language. When using a computer and files of various types, we use words like *save* and *convert*, but also *justify*, for example; saving a text document, converting files of different types of electronic format, justifying the text. These three words are very familiar to theologians,[15] and behind them lies an important intuition, one that is not simply tied to a way of *saying* the faith, but perhaps also to a way of *thinking* it. In this context it is illuminating to look at the theological roots of these terms and compare how they are used in informatics (Forte 2006). It might be still more interesting, though, to understand the impact that recapturing these terms could have on the intelligence of the faith.[16] It is further necessary to understand that it is possible to speak of a "digital intelligence" and detail its characteristics.[17] This is still uncharted territory; the two environments, theology and informatics, certainly seem methodologically to be completely distinct and separate. In any case, the language and the metaphors mold our way of imagining and understanding the general reality. We need a broad anthropological approach to technology to understand what is being discussed. As the writer Michael Fuller—theologian and organic chemist, and the author of *Atoms and Icons*—writes, theologians can look at scientific and technological evolution to understand what it says about our world, and which metaphors and analogies can nourish theological thought (Fuller 1995; 2010).

SAVING, CONVERTING, JUSTIFYING, SHARING

This section is nothing more than an attempt to open a path for reflection.

What does it signify to save a text file, or a photograph, that has just been edited? To save something in the digital world signifies saving it from oblivion, from forgetting, from cancellation. To save, in a theological sense, signifies saving from damnation, from condemnation. Forgiveness is salvation from condemnation. Salvation and forgiveness are terms that seek each other. When saving digital files, salvation is instead the exact opposite of cancellation. If a file is saved, everything, including the errors, is retained. Note that digital saving cancels oblivion. Today, the Web has become the place in which oblivion is impossible, the place in which our traces remain potentially uncancellable. If one wanted to reinvent a new life, the traces of our past would always be there.

To clarify, if a person who has led a dissolute life, dedicated to pornography, decides to turn his life around, his images will continue to exist on the Web, reminding everyone of what he used to be and, in the virtual world, thus will always remain. Digital *saving* (i.e., rescue) of the pornstar, paradoxically coincides with the impossibility of his *pardon*. However, this is only an extreme example. A practical application of what I am talking about is represented, for example, in technology: on opening an email, or visiting certain websites. For example, the email service or website automatically collects some information about the person reading the mail or visiting the website. So "before the difficulty of living in a world without forgiveness, we must . . . find new ways to lose the digital traces that we always leave behind us" (Rosen 2010).

Above all, today more than ever, we understand better how forgiveness does not coincide at all with oblivion and that authentic pardon is an operation that transcends my story and comes out of the system of my possibilities, being founded on God's alterity. In the world in which "my sin stays always before" (Psalms 52.5) and all is digitally saved, how is it still possible to think of religious salvation? This is also the case for conversion. To convert a file signifies changing it into another format. It is a question of coding and thus of language. Digital conversion is a translation of sorts. The conversion of a file can be necessary because the application that we are using cannot *read* or open it. As the user, I cannot relate to the data that it contains because I am unable to decipher the data and have a need to do so and for this reason I convert the file to a format that permits me to enter into a relationship with these data. Conversion is thus the redemption of incommunicability. Can technological conversion have an effect on the comprehension of religious conversions? In this case, if we consider the interesting connotations of opening (to open a file) and the restoration of a communicative relationship (reading a file) that technological conversion involves, we illuminate theological conversion through the original significance of reopening a broken relationship to re-establish a contact that generates sense. *To save* and *to convert* are simply two examples. With the rise of social networks, we can also add *to share* and *community* (Sequeri 2010, 43). The risk of mixing levels becomes easy and the risk that we may fall into a sort of "ideology" of the Web is even larger.[18] In any case, we must be aware that the culture of cyberspace, beyond any other consideration, objectively poses new challenges to our capacity to formulate and hear a symbolic public language that speaks of the possibility of and the signs of transcendence in our lives. The software that "transports atoms of culture"

(Manovich 2010, 14) is, in fact, already the daily bread of millions of people, and the question of language cannot be reduced in any way to that of the provisional "coating" of concepts that are always equal and identical to themselves.[19]

The choice of language to which I have referred is only the first level of reflection. How, in the fullest manner, does digital culture shape the way we form a discourse on God and the faith, especially if this discourse is specifically Catholic?

Until now, discussions on religion and the Web have largely focused on cyberreligion,[20] techno-agnosticism, and technopaganism[21]—in short, these discussions have paid more attention to the *religious* than to the *theological* dimension, at the risk of flattening and approving specific identities and theologies when these identities and theologies should no longer be subjected to this homogenizing, sociological approach. Certainly, the fact that several forms of virtual religiosity have been born on the Web is the epiphenomenon of a complex and ample change in the comprehension of the sacred (Schroeder, Heather, and Lee 1998). Nevertheless, it is not sufficient to stop there (Pace and Giordan 2010, 761–81). In reality, reflection on cybertheology is in its early stages, but its epistemology is as yet uncertain. The term *cybertheological reflection*, in fact, is rarely used, and often its sense is not obvious. The question, instead, is clear: if the electronic media and digital technologies "modify the way of communicating and even that of thinking, what impact will they have on the way we do theology?" (Berger 1996, 195). The first timid and rapid attempts to arrive at a definition have in reality sought to clarify the terms under which the questions are asked.

Susan George (2006, 182) has gathered four definitions of cybertheology as examples of possible understandings. The first definition is framed as the theology of the meanings of social communication in the era of the Internet and of advanced technologies. The second is understood as a pastoral reflection on how to communicate the Gospel through the Web's own capacity. The third definition she interprets as a phenomeno-logical map of the presence of the religious on the Internet. The fourth one, on how to trawl the Web, is understood as a place with spiritual capacities. Her approach is an interesting first attempt to define a field for reflection. The English theologian Debbie Herring has distinguished three sections: "theology in," "theology of," and "theology for" cyberspace.[22] The first collects theological materials that are available on the Web; the second offers a list of theological contributions to the study of cyberspace; the third consists of a collection of places in which one can form theology on the Web (forums, sites, mailing lists). These distinctions are interesting and provide some key clarification that enriches reflection on theology in cyberspace.

Carlo Formenti (2008, 59–107) refers to cybertheology as the study of the theological connotations of technoscience, a "theol-ogy of technology." George, by contrast, tends to keep technol-ogy and theology separate. The monograph fascicle of the journal *Concilium* (2005)—entitled "Cyber-spazio, cyber-etica, cyber-teologia" (Cyber-space, cyber-ethics, cyber-theology)—implic-itly seems to define cybertheology as the study of spirituality expressed on the Internet and of the everyday representation and imagination of the sacred. Consequently, this deals with reflections on changes in the relationships with God and tran-scendence. In this book, I seek a new status, a more precise one, for this discipline that seems so difficult to define. It is necessary to consider cybertheology as being the intelligence of the faith in the era of the Internet, that is, reflection on the thinkability of the faith in the light of the Web's logic. This refers to reflec-tion that is born from the question about the mode in which the Web's logic—with its powerful metaphors that work on the imaginary, beyond intelligence—can model the listening to and reading of the Bible. It can also model the ways of under-standing the classical themes of systematic theology: the Church and ecclesial communion, Revelation, liturgy, the sacraments.

Reflection is more important than ever, because it is easy to note how the Internet increasingly helps shape people's identities in general and those of "digital natives" in particular (Lövheim and Linderman 2005, 121–37).

Cybertheological reflection is always a reflexive knowledge that starts from the experience of faith. This becomes theology in the sense that it responds to the *formula fides quarens intellectum*. Cybertheology is not, therefore, a sociological reflection on religiosity on the Internet, but is the fruit of faith that frees from itself a cognitive impulse at a time when the Web's logic marks the way of thinking, knowing, communicating, and living.

Perhaps I should emphasize that it is not sufficient to consider cybertheological reflection as one of the many cases of "contextual theology," which holds cybertheological reflection in a specific manner in the human context in which it is expressed. At present, this is certainly the case. However, the Web cannot be simply isolated as a specific and determinate case from our everyday lives but has to be seen as an integral part of our ordinary existence.[23] Digital culture claims to connect people with one another, opening up new relationships (Spadaro 2010). Of course, this is not without ambiguities. A society that is based on a web of connections poses significant challenges, not just for the pastoral—which the Church has accepted already for some time[24]—but also for the comprehension of the Christian faith itself, starting with its use of language. The image that perhaps illustrates the role and claims of Christianity before digital culture is that of the carver of the sycamores, borrowed from the prophet Amos (7.14) and interpreted by St. Basil. The then Cardinal Ratzinger, in his discourse at the Media Parables Conference, used this fortunate image to say that Christianity is like a cut on a fig.[25] The sycamore tree produces a lot of insipid fruit that remains inedible if not treated properly. For St. Basil, the fruit or figs represent the culture of his time. The Christian Logos is a cut that permits culture to mature, and the cut requires wisdom, because it is done well at the correct moment. Digital culture is rich with fruit to press and the Christian is called to undertake the work of mediating between the Logos and digital culture. This work is not without challenges, but nonetheless demands our attention. In particular, we must begin to think about the Web theologically, but also about the theology in the Web's logic. The first question is: what faith do we find in the anthropological space that is the Web?

CHAPTER 2

The Human Being
Decoder and Search Engine for God

Walk through any major city and you will see numerous people with earphones (AKA earbuds). It hasn't been that long since we had become accustomed to seeing adolescents and young people with Walkman devices in their hands or bags. Today the iPod and other digital music players have taken its place, making it possible for people to listen to music anywhere, even while exercising. One might ask, and rightly so, if this convenience might not also contribute to one's losing touch with ordinary reality, and whether it causes an acoustic isolation that impedes those simple and banal occasions for dialogue and listening that (used to?) punctuate a person's dayly experiences: "Excuse me . . ."; "Please . . ."; "Can you tell me the time?"; "Can you tell me the way to . . . ?"; "Where can I find . . . ?" Putting on ear- or headphones is a way of shielding ourselves from the everyday noise that surrounds us and changing our relationship with our environment by introducing our own soundtrack. The normal social activities that used to occur appear to be disrupted. The phenomenon is not only understood in negative terms. The creation of an acoustic, mobile environment can make one's daily routine less repetitive and monotonous, and can help make a relaxing walk more enjoyable. However, it certainly introduces a different way of experiencing life.[1]

MUSIC AS SPACE

What people are listening to has nothing to do with faith, because "faith is born from listening and listening relates to the words of Christ" (Letter to the Romans 10.17). Listening has been the hinge of faith since the invitation "Hear, O Israel! The Lord is our God, the Lord alone" (Deuteronomy 6.4). Here, God not only reveals himself in his irreducible difference when compared to every other divinity, but reveals himself as he who seeks a profound relationship with man, which implies heart, mind, and strength. The voice of God calls the individual of faith who is, above all, a "hearer of the Word," as mentioned. Now, the iPod, in modifying the way we listen, can modify the logic of listening that has nothing to do with faith.[2] Perhaps the first consideration is that the iPod permits us to carry with us all of our music and to listen to it in any situation. Listening is no longer principally an activity, but the start of a soundtrack to everything that we make. We no longer listen when we do things and take music for granted as background "noise." All the steps that were a prerequisite to listening to music in the past— taking a disc, turning on a record player, putting the needle in its place, and so on—have been reduced to a simple action: pressing a button, even without the need to establish what to hear. However, listening is no longer an action of *obedience* (*ob audire*), but of *accompaniment*, which does not give meaning but emotion to the things that we do. Listening creates an environment rather than communicating a message.[3]

MISSING OBEDIENCE

To this form of experience can be added a modality that is specific to listening to music: so-called shuffle listening, from which the iPod Shuffle derives its name. This particular iPod model permits us to listen to songs randomly chosen by the device. The verb "to shuffle" signifies "to mix"; and it is commonly used for shuffling cards. Apple has transformed this philosophy of listening to music into a lifestyle, coining an influential publicity slogan that expresses a beautiful idea crystallized into a concept of destiny, providence, and will: "Life is random" (Sofri 2005). Sociologists and commentators have affirmed that the apparent irrationality of the iPod Shuffle is perfectly aligned to a condition of life that is characterized by improvisation, by the casual furnishing of sensations, of flexibility. Does a philosophy of life of this type give value to the experience of life or does it mortify it? This is similar to the idea that if every experience is casual—without sense, precarious, incomprehensible, and fleeting—then it can become an obstacle to a life lived in its fullness. In reality, this can also surprise, enabling a taste for the unexpected or the unawaited approach. In fact, often the iPod is loaded with a lot of music of which the title and author are not always known. The iPod was subsequently given a key, called VoiceOver, which, if pressed while listening to one's favorite music, shows the title and the artist. We listen to music as a background to our environment and then, if something draws our attention, we activate the decoder. Beyond every valuation and beyond the resistance that it is necessary to put before the widespread deafness toward a message that requires specific and willing listening, certainly the faith *ex auditu* must count on an ability to listen to the environment and the shuffle that does not provide for a specific time of hearing, but for widespread listening that is able to accompany our lives, rather than asking for our attention.

THE FAITH SUPERMARKET

In the context of listening and shuffling, where the human being is a type of decoder of messages, what traits does the search for God—which traditionally involves pausing, silence, and listening—assume? Today search is, in reality, one of the most lived practices on the Web, and religiosity is involved in it. How would seeking God manifest itself in the era of search engines?[4] Typing into Google the word *God*—or *religion*, *Christ*, or *spirituality*—returns a list of hundreds of millions of pages. On the Web, one becomes aware of a growth of religious needs that religious tradition has difficulty satisfying. Individuals today are inclined to read about religion on the Web, to talk about religious topics, to download religious texts and documents, to buy religious objects, to undertake indexed search for sacred texts, to produce tours of virtual churches, to find religious centers, to assist in various types of prayers and worship, to listen to religious music, homilies, prayers, witnessing, speeches, to take part in virtual pilgrimages, and so on. The common opinion that our technologized world has no space for spirituality is clearly refuted. The individual in search of God today uses technically advanced instruments and factual data (Teusner 2008). What are the consequences? We might fool ourselves into believing that the sacred and religious are just a click away. The Web—thanks to its ability to contain and provide access to all kinds of information—can easily be compared to a type of big supermarket of the religious, in which it is possible to find every type of religious "product, of the most serious and valid reflections on religions that a bored person invents as a game, is easy. Each may draw from the Web, not according to real spiritual exigencies, but to satisfy needs. We deceive ourselves, when we actually believe that the sacred remains 'at the disposition' of a 'consumer' at the moment of need" (Roof 1999).

To understand the danger of religious homogenization, there are sites, such as Beliefnet, where religions are put on show, paired with each other, in an often disarming cocktail.[5] Scanning these sites and the instruments that they put at our disposal, one can gain a glimpse of the profound need for God that stirs man's heart.

THE DECODING HUMAN AND "ORBITAL" CONTENT

In this context, however, we need to consider a possible radical change in the perception of the question of religion. At one time, the human being used to be attracted by the religious as a source of fundamental sense and orientation. Then the human being invented the compass, and that device implies that there is a unique and precise reference point. Next, the human being substituted the compass with radar, which implies an indiscriminate opening even to the blandest signals, and at times this is not without the perception of "turning to the void." The human being, though, was understood as a "listener to the Word," in search of a message for which he/she felt a profound need. Today, these images, even if still alive and true, pertain less. Or, better, if once upon a time radar sought a signal, today one seeks a channel of access through which data can pass. This happens also in the search for a Wi-Fi signal, or at least for a smartphone data connection. Humans today, more than seeking a signal, are used to seeking so as to always have the possibility of receiving a signal without, though, having to seek them. The extreme consequence is that of the logic introduced by the push system, which works in a way opposite to that of the pull system. The first implies that when a piece of data is available (an e-mail, for example) I receive it automatically because I keep a reception channel open.

The second system implies that I can recover it when I want to establish a connection. The human being—first through the aid of the compass and then radar—is being transformed into a decoder. We are bombarded by messages in our daily lives; we suffer from a so-called information overload. The problem today is not to find the message that makes sense, but to decode it, to recognize it on the basis of the multiple messages that we receive. Increasingly, digital witnessing to faith becomes "accounting for hope" (1 Pt 3.15) in a context in which reason is quickly and wildly being confronted. "Making its way" is the classic mechanism of advertising, which offers answers to questions that have not yet been formulated. In reality, the religious question is being transformed into a confrontation between answers that are plausible and those that are subjectively significant.

The great word to rediscover, then, has long been part of the Christian vocabulary: discernment. We never lack radical questions, but today they are mediated by so-called filtered and tailored search returns that we receive. These returns are the place from which the question emerges. We must learn, deduce and distinguish the truly religious questions from the replies that are continually given (Benedict XVI 2012).

According to this logic, then, this is not about the question, but about the religious answer, and this is dependent of the fact that the Web molds the way we understand the content of faith, which becomes content that orbits around those who seek or find it. This orbital dimension is another characteristic that the Web is taking on. In fact, services, bookmark, and read later applications (such as Instapaper, Pocket, Watch It Later, Gimme Bar, Spool) allow us to save the content that we find on the Web, and in which we are interested, in a unique virtual place and in a standard format, in such a way that it is possible to access it at a later moment, at times even while offline. How many times have we come across some interesting articles or videos while surfing the Web without having had the time to be able to consume them all at once? Until a short time ago, in order to save them from oblivion it was necessary to bookmark the Web address. Now, instead, as soon as we find some interesting content we can have it orbit around us, totally abstracted from its context, saving it thanks to an application. The content becomes "orbital content" (Koczon 2011).

The logic of Instapaper and other similar applications is that the data that result from my searches are "fished" from the Web, selected for their interest, taken away from their roots, and are made to converge on a platform that saves them in such a way that it is possible to postpone reading them until a later time.

We thus develop the sense that knowledge is called to orbit around us in a way that is completely functional to and oriented toward us. Today, the faith seems to participate in this logic, that is, as a way to manage complexity. We can therefore jump the hierarchically constituted schedules, as happened in traditional broadcasting, in favor of podcasting and YouTube channels. What can we conclude from this? Many human beings have a need to recognize their desire for God in the messages that reach us. They have a need to be helped to identify which are the answers that really give sense to their existence in its totality, and they have a need to find in themselves a strong spiritual center that is able to give unity to the fragmentation of the messages that strike them profoundly.

THE GOSPEL AND GOODS

In a context in which the human being is a decoder of messages that contain meaning and that orbit the subject, what is the Gospel? The Word of the Gospel cannot be considered "a line on the table next to another one," but as "the key, a message that has a nature totally different from much of the information under which we are submerged day after day."[6] Rather, from this message's characteristics, the questions depend on the correct form of its communication. If the Gospel appears only as one piece of news among many, it can perhaps be discarded in favor of other, more important messages, or those that orbit around the subject in such a way that it becomes one among many sources of wisdom. How is it that the communication that Christians call the Gospel can be understood in a form that is totally other from information, however? This is a serious task, because it marks the demarcation between faith as goods that can be sold in a seductive manner, and faith as an act of the intelligence of man who, moved by God, gives his own assent to Him freely.

Someone of Christian faith is neither a consumer of religious services, nor someone who holds an answer. Christianity understands itself to be the carrier of a message—that of the death and resurrection of Christ. This message resists assimilation; it is scandalous; it attempts to answer human kind's questions. The Christian presence on the Web must use the fact that the Word of the Gospel disturbs the conscience. It does not calm or satisfy; it is not there to make life better. On the contrary, it could cause a serious crisis of conscience, or, one might even say, make you sick. The way to confront that dialectical intersection is "by a shrewd game of spontaneity and reticence, transparency and the simulation of the chance of public exposure and the custody of intimacy that is otherwise inaccessible" (Sequeri 2001, 11), inside a marketplace that is already saturated with messages. Today, it is necessary to realize that there are realities that can always escape, whatever the algorithm of the search engine, and so the "googlization" of the faith is impossible because it is false.

THE SEARCH FOR MEANING

Google has introduced a new search feature called Instant, which shows search results as you type. A useful innovation that was born from an observation: "Users type slowly, but they are able to read a lot more quickly: normally, in fact, between one stroke and another on the keyboard there is a gap of 300 milliseconds, but one needs only 30 milliseconds (a tenth of the time) to glance at another section of the page."[7] Google technicians have calculated that this new feature helps save at least two to five seconds per search, collectively about eleven million seconds her hour if all of those who use search engines instead used Instant.

It is also true, as the Google Instant search page explains, that it is possible to modify one's search instantly, if the results that are returned do not correspond exactly to what we want to find. Even if we don't know exactly which search term to type in, the search engine tries to predict it for us to help guide our search. The top predictions are shown in grey text in the search box, so you can stop typing as soon as you see the desired search term.

Google Instant saves us time and gives us a more refined search option. However, this benefit comes at a price. Searches conducted by Google Instant show that the potential search term is already a given. We no longer need to type it out. The results also are made more precise by digitalization, but the results of such research are therefore skewed according to the search engine's criteria and what it presumes to be the user's preferences.[8]

For example, if we type in the word *God*, we discover that in the Google marketplace of returns, the answer to God is certainly no longer "the being than whom you can think of no greater," according to the definition of St. Anselm. In fact, for me, the automatic suggestions in the English language that appear as soon as I enter the letters g, o, and d are, in order, "Godaddy," "God of War," and "God of Metal," which are, respectively, an Internet service provider company, a videogame, and a heavy metal music festival. God as such is not part of the list of possible search terms in my example. For this reason, it has been written—ironically—that the search for God in the Google Instant era has been made difficult.[9] Somebody amused him- or herself by furnishing the proof that Google itself is God.[10] Obviously, any innovation that is capable of improving search on the Web can only be welcomed, but we need to reflect on the possible consequences that these functions end up having on man's most profound attitudes, especially when we express a desire for transcendence.

The logic of the instantaneous search engine should be compared with the logic of semantic search engines. Take, for example, Wolfram|Alpha, a computing knowledge engine, which is an engine that decodes and processes, weaving together data for its own purposes: key words are inserted by the user and it immediately offers a response to them. Since, at the moment, the only language that it understands is English, it is interesting to note that the answer to the question (in English): "Does

God exist?" is "I'm sorry, but a poor computational knowledge engine, no matter how powerful, is not capable of providing a simple answer to that question."[11] Where a search engine like Google can furnish hundreds and thousands of indirect answers, Wolfram|Alpha takes a step back. The difference is that a syntactic search engine, such as Google, is uniquely concerned with the actual words that are within a text, without any way to attempt to determine the context in which these words are being used. By contrast, semantic search tends to approximate the way human beings think, seeking to interpret the logical significance of the phrases and to understand the significance in context. In a cultural context in which a sensible response tends to precede the question, it is important to learn to formulate questions well, considering that the search for God is always semantic, and its significance is never abstract and always depends on a context.

CHAPTER 3

The Mystical and Connective Body

The Internet connects people. Online, however, everyone can create his or her own fictitious and simulated identity, begging the question how much faith can we put in online identities and relationships? What are the risks? On the Web, everyone can fool others into believing that he/she is someone else with regard to his or her age, gender, or profession. On the Web, you can become the message. In short, you converse as what or who you feel you are, and for no other reason than to express yourself.

THE WEB IS A HOT PLACE

It is for this reason that, potentially, the Web imparts confidence, because it permits us to say things that are difficult for a person to say in his or her everyday physical context. One can totally expose oneself—in a premeditated or spontaneous fashion—without limits and shame. Cyberspace is, to paraphrase McLuhan, a place that is emotively *hot*, and not technologically frozen as some are tempted to imagine. Certainly, it is enough to disconnect oneself, or to close an application, in order to shut down a relationship. In some cases, however, the Web is "broken" and people meet with each other in a real space. The gradual transition from static web pages to dynamic or user-generated content and the growth of social networks—generally referred to as Web 2.0—have allowed us to understand how relationships between people are at the center of the system and content exchange.[1] Before Facebook and similar social networks, the Web focused largely on content. People could contact each other, join newsgroups, or sign up for mailing lists; human relationships themselves, however, were largely invisible. Today, by contrast, relationships between humans are at the center. Social networks are not an ensemble of individuals, but an ensemble of relationships between individuals. They include ways for different social networking platforms to interact with each other. The key concept is no longer merely *presence* on the Web but *connection*. If we are present, but not connected, we are alone.[2] We enter the Web to experiment, or to add to some form of proximity. We must thus have a good understanding of how the concept of the "proximate" itself—and, more specifically, of friendship—changes and evolves due to the Web itself. Furthermore, social networks worldwide are not just limited to Facebook and Twitter. Many others exist—some based on geography, others based on ethnic backgrounds, and still others based on more narrow interests of their members.[3] These social networks help to develop widespread relationships, even allowing entry to groups whose origins are based on different interests and backgrounds than one's own.

All social networking platforms can both help and threaten relationships. Human relationships are not simply a game, and they need time and awareness to develop. The Web's mediated relationships are always necessarily incomplete; people may not always be aware of each other's true personality, even looks. Benedict XVI (2009b) wrote:

It would be sad if our desire to sustain and develop friendships online were realized at the cost of the availability of the family, of neighbors and those we encounter in everyday reality, in our workplaces, at school, in our free time, When, in fact, the desires for virtual connection become obsessive, the consequence is that the person isolates themselves, breaking real social interaction. This also ends by disturbing their models of rest, of silence and of reflection, which are necessary for healthy, human development.

If the Web, despite its promise of connecting people, ends up isolating people, then it betrays itself and its significance. The crux of the problem is that connecting and sharing on the Web are not the same as meeting someone in person, which requires an effort to sustain and make a relationship work.

WHO IS MY NEIGHBOR?

The fruit of this betrayal, that is, of possible separations between connecting and meeting, between sharing and relationships, was suggested in the title of a work by the psychoanalyst Luigi Zoja (2009): *La morte del prossimo* (The death of the neighbor). Paradoxically, relationships can be maintained without giving up our own condition of egotistical isolation. Rather, our so-called real friends—just because they are always online (read: available for contact) or are imagined to be present while glancing at our updates on social networks—risk becoming a projection of our imagination. Italo Calvino (1994) had a very good intuition, in reference to the telephone, about the possible consequences of distance relationships, when he wrote in his story "Prima che tu dica 'Pronto'" ("Before you say 'Hello'"):

> Until I am by your side the distance is unbridgeable. However, it is just for this reason that I do not see the time to call you, because only in a long distance telephone call, or better an international one, can we hope to reach that way of being that is usually defined as "being together." . . . I leave to call you every day, because I have always been there for you, and you always for me, at the other end

of the line. . . . And when this line is not between us to establish contact, when our own rough, physical presence occupies the sensory field, immediately all that is between us becomes known again, superfluous, automatic . . . in short, our presence will be a beautiful thing for both of us but you certainly cannot compare it with the frequency of vibrations that pass through the electronic switching of large telephone networks and with the intensity of emotions that it can provoke in us.

Instead, the concept of the neighbor is not hung on a wire, but has its roots in and is tied to spatial proximity. The fracturing of proximity comes from the immediacy of technological mediation; whoever is *connected* to or *near* me is also *not near* my friend, who lives close by but does not use e-mail or Facebook (see Brasher 2004, 116–19). Instead I feel *close* to somebody because she has become a *friend*, since she is the friend of a friend, with whom I have frequent exchanges online.

This estrangement is deeply rooted in the anonymity of the mass media. Until the beginning of the twentieth century, the majority of the population lived in an agricultural environment and people certainly knew no more than a few hundred faces in their whole lives. Today, it is normal not to recognize the faces we meet in the street, and it is painfully obvious that the neighbor is someone unknown. The problematic that results is that one comes to value proximity through criteria that are too elementary, without the complexity that a true, deep relationship has. Technology makes the brain ever more susceptible to experience relationships similar to a videogame, which is based on a right answer/wrong answer logic, to the stimuli that I send to the other person. In a Christian way, however, the neighbor is certainly not the person who offers the right answer to our stimuli to him or her. The Gospel's logic is very clear in this respect:

> For if you love those who love you, what credit is that to you? Even sinners love those who love them.
>
> And if you do good to those who do good to you, what credit is that to you? Even sinners do the same

> If you lend money to those from whom you expect repayment, what credit (is) that to you? Even sinners lend to sinners, and get back the same amount.
>
> But rather, love your enemies and do good to them, and lend expecting nothing back; then your reward will be great and you will be children of the Most High, for he himself is kind to the ungrateful and the wicked.
>
> Be merciful, just as (also) your Father is merciful. (Luke 6.32–35)

In today's context, when Luke, the evangelist, speaks of "doing good," this has to be read in the most literal way possible. People increasingly contact each other through online gaming communities using *words*, that is, stories and written messages. Not too long ago, for example, for the young to be friends, this was possible only if they participated in a shared activity: for example, going out for pizza, playing music together, or joining a club. Today, it is possible to be friends simply by writing about one's own life on an electronic bulletin board. Constructing friendships in the era of the Web therefore signifies dealing with more possibilities for contact, but it also requires a greater awareness of the intensity and profundity that is possible in "incarnated" human relationships.

WHERE IS MY NEIGHBOR?

What seems to have been lost in our connected times—the interest in real, physical contact with people and friends—is beginning to reemerge in other forms and through other means. Considering the fact that today the streets are a place for anonymous proximity, one may ask oneself how is it possible to maintain a close relationship with one's friends given how busy our lives have become, especially for urban dwellers. This possibility has been recovered thanks to the geolocation feature supported by smartphones. In 2009, the location-based social networks Foursquare and Gowalla were born. In 2010, Facebook promoted the Places feature.

These location-based services share a simple premise: when you are in a place, you *check in* with your smartphone—that is you signal your presence—which makes you visible to those who are your friends (real or virtual) and who you have allowed to see your location on a map. In this way, the virtual and the physical worlds are connected and, potentially, the connection can become a chance encounter. Checking in signals your presence in a place and effectively announces that you are available to meet up, have a cup of coffee together, or just say hello. Google Latitude radicalized this concept of geolocalized publicity by allowing the smartphone user to be located anywhere and to be traceable by people who are empowered to do so.

Without detailed analysis of all of the characteristics, even the eminently ludic ones, of these location-based social networks, we can ask ourselves what is encouraging people to continually violate their own personal privacy and to communicate their own movements to their digital worlds. This, of course, expresses a need for proximity, that is, a desire to carry the world of their own relationships to a *real* level of contact. In a world where the lack of physical proximity and busy work schedules make it increasingly difficult to find oneself among familiar faces, one seeks to pull the threads of the Web with the help of an application that tells us of an opportunity to meet some nearby friend with a little free time in the place in which one happens to be at this point in time. In the meantime, one also takes note of other places of interest close by (according to the social networking application, of course) that are currently *trending* because of the presence of the greatest number of people who have checked in.

Location-based social networks introduce a *fluid* version of proximity, which is based on the concept of the local. The idea of the public space is moved to the territory of the smartphone itself. It is the application that tells us whether we can meet and where, permitting us to puncture the anonymity of the environment that surrounds us. The idea of a local church must, sooner or later, take this vision of relationships into account. Will the local church tend to be a geolocalized church, whose membership will be linked forever to its network of reference, which moves in that territory? To create occasions for communal prayer, will we approach the check-in at a place of worship, a church? Sharing one's whereabouts could be a factor that, sooner or later, will have an impact on the way we build ecclesial communities, just like the evolution of our means of transportation transformed communities over time.[4]

A FLUID CHURCH?

If we accept the concept of the *proximate being*, how can we imagine the future of life in an ecclesial community in the era of the Web? What will be the characteristics of the church of the so-called Generation Y, that is, the young who were born between 1980 and the early 2000s?[5] The territorial reference *fluid*, and the lack of a shared life, will surely end in compromising a truly significant relationality. There is no need, though, to be silent about some of the positive aspects, such as the spontaneous aggregation of sensitivities and elective commonalities. However, a community cannot be absolutely mediated in a determinate manner by a sophisticated technology. Very often, meetings between people are mediated by technology: the car, the bus, the cell phone, text messages, and so on. They are technological instruments that make meetings, or even the frequency of the sacraments, possible, but they are widespread and easy to access. At the moment, this is not true for the most sophisticated digital technologies. Technological barriers should be considered equal to architectonic ones. In a web community we risk avoiding comparison with and between the differences of age, culture, jobs, ideas, and sensitivities. Like any other form of marketing, one might over-segment pastoral care to appeal to a particular community sector: care of the young, the family, the elderly, the sick, and so on. Think of the so-called churches generated by televangelists which produce individual religious practices that confirm the exasperated privatization of life's purposes and of the extreme individualism of capitalist consumer society, for which the motto is: "every man for himself and God for all." Is this not due to chance and the success of websites that spread spirituality, free from any form of historical mediation, community, or sacramental forms (such as tradition, testimony, celebration, and so on) that tend to include all religious values uniquely in the consciousness of the individual, often inspired by a new age sensibility?

Such tensions evidently raise the meaning of church membership. The risk arises that such tensions are considered to be a consensus that is the result of communication. In this context, the steps of Christian initiation risk being resolved into a sort of access procedure (or log-in)—perhaps also on the basis of a contract of sorts—that permits rapid disconnection (log-off). The roots of a community are resolved into an installation (set-up) of an application (software) on a machine (hardware) that one can also remove again (uninstall).[6]

Without experience, today we believe that we can always turn back; this we reduce to a simple experiment. Simulation beats the real by its greater potentiality and its low risk level. This has consequences that are both emotive and affective. In a world that may frighten us, a good game has everything that is simulated, giving us the illusion that we are in control and undesired outcomes can be reversed. The true problem is therefore given by the reduction of reality to a representation that we can manipulate, that is, it is reversible, through which experience is reduced to simulation, an interactive game, the fruition of an image. The more the simulation gratifies and engages, the more addictive it is, and the more it depends on simulation, as the relationships within them evaporate and with them all forms of real relationship with what is other to me and goes beyond my desires or fears. In short, then, the relationships with the people playing the games would be more valued. The challenge that is on the horizon is alienation, the refuge of a fictional, painless world that makes us lose contact with the incomparable wealth of irreversible experiences.

More and more, the Web will not be a parallel, separate world distinct from everyday reality and direct two-dimensional contacts, on- and offline. These contacts should be, as much as possible, harmonized and integrated into a life of full, sincere relationships. The Church in itself always includes more (and remains understandable) in terms of its networks (McLuhan 1999, 83).[7]

THE CHURCH AS A HUB?

In his book *Thy Kingdom Connected*, Dwight J. Friesen (2009, 31) imagines "the Kingdom of God in terms of beings who are relationally connected with God, one with the others, and with all of creation." In this vision, we can certainly find again that of the *Compendium of the Catechism of the Catholic Church*, which affirms that the sacramentality of the Church is in its being "the instrument of reconciliation and of communion for all of humanity with God and of the unity of all of mankind."[8] Friesen's thought expresses a vision of the Church itself—actually of the so-called emerging Church—as a broad movement that is complex and fluid in the charismatic, evangelical area, and which will plant the Christian faith again in the new, post-Christian context. This goes beyond the individual Christian confessions and is characterized by the rejection of the so-called solid ecclesial structures. Instead, a lot of emphasis is put on relational paradigms, on all the expressions that—according to Zygmunt Bauman—can be defined as the equivalent of community, on unpublished approaches and highly creative spirituality, and to worship.[9] This results in a church that is "organic, interconnected, decentralized, constructed from the bottom up, flexible, and always evolving" (Brewin 2007, 58).

In this picture, it seems that the nature and mystery of the Church is being diluted into becoming a "connective space," a hub of connections that supports a "connective authority" (Friesen 2009, 80) and whose purpose is mainly to connect people. The metaphor chosen, the model, is Google. Friesen, in fact, writes that Google helps us to understand better connective leaders because the famous search engine is not in itself the information that we seek, but is what connects us to what we seek. Nobody goes to the Google website just to visit the site; people go to the Google site to find what is sought. Friesen concludes that "this connective vision (networked) of leadership is vital in order to understand who will be the connective leader and what relational authority will be used in a connective relational vision (networked) of the world" (81). Google's authority is not intrinsic, but is something that the search engine company has earned, sending its users the connections that it can establish. This is the connective authority of Google: its capacity to put us in touch with information. Friesen concludes that "the 'Google parable' can be useful in thinking more biblically of the nature and function of Christian leadership in the Churches, in organizations, in activities, and in families" (81). The notion of the Church that emerges from this vision is that of a networked church (Whitsitt 2011), which rethinks and understands the structures of local churches. These become Christ Commons, whose primary purpose is to create and develop a connective environment where it is easy for people to regroup (or cluster) in the name of Christ. To understand this idea, it is important to understand two key concepts: that of the *common* and that of the *cluster*. The common is a public space like, for example, a town square or a public garden. An example is Boston Common, the oldest public park in the United States. This term is used to indicate other things of a so-called common character. In particular, on the Web, the expression is well known because it indicates a typology of licences that permit those who retain the copyright to transmit some of them to the public and to keep others. It means, for example, being able to distribute an original text without having the right to change it, or to distribute it to draw an economic profit. It is, therefore, a license that allows sharing without the typical restrictions of a classic copyright. All of this feeds into the idea of the Christ Common, that is, "a visible structure, something like an institution, a denomination, a building, a celebration, a small group that is formally created with the hope of a structure that constitutes an environment, or a space, where people can have an experience of a life in connection with God and with others" (107). Manuel Castells (2003, 127), the well-known scholar of the information society, understood this well when he wrote:

> The key question for us is the journey of the community to the network as the central form of organizational interaction. Communities, at least in the tradition of sociological research, were based on sharing values and social organization. Networks are made up of the choices and strategies of social actors, whether they are individuals, families or groups.

In this vision, the Church will therefore be a support structure—a hub, a square—where people can cluster, giving life to clusters of connections. The term *cluster* has its equivalent in the telematics world, because it identifies a computer ensemble connected across a Web. The purpose of a cluster is to spread very complex processes among the various computers that are part of its makeup. This obviously augments the system's computing power. The Church as Christ Common is not, therefore, a place of reference. It is not a lighthouse that emits light but a support structure. Its objective is not to increase the number of its members but to increase the Kingdom of God. From this perspective, we do not exclude the "pastors, heads, bishops, the pope, or other" (114), but we understand them as a network, as ecologists, people who have the duty to keep the functions of the Web inside a society that is founded on a form of neonomadism thanks to which relationships can be reconfigured with minimum inertia (Lévy 1997a, 31). This vision offers an idea of the Christian community that makes the characteristics of a virtual community itself turn into light, without historical constraints, and which is geographically fluid. Certainly, this horizontality helps us greatly to understand the Church's mission, which is to evangelize. In effect, all of the formulation of emerging ecclesiology is strongly missionary. In this sense, it gives value to connective capacity and witnessing. On the other hand, it seems that the comprehension of the Church as the "mystic body," which is diluted into a sort of platform of connections, moves further away.

VINE BRANCHES OR INTERNET WIRES?

An event that made me reflect critically on the connective vision of the Church was not taking a theological position but looking at a lay event: how the Internal Revenue Service (IRS) of the United States defines a church.[10] The IRS, for the purpose of tax exemption, has sought to define what qualifies as a church in an objective way, based on characteristics that can be easily recognized. According to the IRS, an institution qualifies as a church (and thus is tax-exempt) if it has:

A distinct legal existence
A recognized creed
A formal code of doctrine and discipline
A defined and distinct ecclesiastical government
A formalized doctrinal code and discipline
An autonomous religious history
A membership that is not associated with any other church or denomination
Ordained ministers, who must be selected after having completed prescribed studies
Its own literature
Its own established places of worship
A regular community
Regular religious services
Sunday schools for the religious instruction of the young.
Schools for the preparation of its ministers.

Given that the connective churches do not answer to these criteria, they, in the eyes of the IRS, cannot be considered churches in the proper sense.[11] This vision of a church that has been expressed by the IRS has engendered many arguments. Beyond all judgment, we understand all too well how the Web, just by virtue of its existence, challenges standard conceptions of how a church community or congregation (and its history) is to be understood.

Lumen Gentium no. 6, speaking of the intimate nature of the Church, affirms that this is made known through "various imagery." In the past, images of other types, including biblical ones, were also used to signify the Church such as naval and navigational metaphors (Rahner 1971). Some images can, in fact, also be ecclesiological models. By *model* we understand an image that is employed in a reflexive and critical way in order to deepen the comprehension of reality (Dulles 1987). To this point, the question is whether today the need has not arisen to confront seriously the figure of the network and what comes from it at the level of ecclesiological understanding. Is it possible to think of the Internet as a metaphor through which to understand the Church, naturally without believing that this can be exhaustive?

Of course, the relational network functions if links are always active; if a node or link were to be discontinued, then information would not pass and the relationship would be impossible. The reticularity of the vine, whose branches flow with the same sap, is not all that distant from the image of the Internet. We can understand that the Web is an image of the Church as a body that is alive if all of the relationships within it are vital. Furthermore, the Church's universality and its mission of proclamation "to all the people" reinforce the perception that the Web can be a good model with ecclesiological value. However, some unanswered questions remain. The principles are based on the fact that the Web can be understood as a sort of great, self-referencing text, and thus as being purely *horizontal*. It has neither roots nor branches, and therefore represents a model that is closed within itself (De Carli 1997). The Church, instead, is not as much a Web of immanent relationships as it is a cluster; yet it always has an *external* principle and foundation. This is combined with its vocation to be part of the Body of Christ, that is the Church. The Church is thus not reducible to a cluster (the sociological model of aggregation), and according to the Catholic vision, the Church is not just a hub. Instead, it is "to designate the people that God called to gather from all corners of the earth, to build an assembly of them, for the faith and for baptism, to become the sons of God, the members of Christ and the temple of the Holy Spirit."[12] The membership of the Church is given this external foundation, because it is Christ who, by means of the Spirit, unites Himself intimately with its faithful; it is He who unites with Himself the Church in an external alliance, making it holy (Ephesians 5.26).[13] The Church, therefore, cannot be reduced to a public space, a common, where people can meet in Christ's name, but is the place of appeal—for a call or vocation—that can also go beyond the limits of a real, pure, and simple will for aggregation. If relationships on the Web depend on the presence and effective functioning of the instruments of communication,[14] ecclesial communion is radically a "gift" of the Spirit. It is in this gift that the Church's communicative action has its basis and its origins (see Canobbio 2001).

THE OPENING OF AN "ISLAND OF SENSE"

Beyond every valuation, we must commence from the notion that there is no technological extension of the human physical capacity that cannot have an impact on the social sphere.

We must therefore take account of a fact and of an expression of human sociality that always puts more value on connections, with superficial contacts, at least as a basis for further investigation. In today's context, Karl Rahner's words become illuminating and current when he affirms that every realization of human society, even an embryonic one, is always an extensive and widespread realization of the Church. In fact, "man is not the being of intercommunication in a marginal manner only but, rather, with this quality he determines the length and breadth of his existence." If "salvation affects the whole man, this puts him in relation to God in his totality and in all of the dimensions of his existence," then "with what has been said, this inter-humanity is also characterized by the Christian religion," which is conceived as an "ecclesial religion" (Rahner 1978, 389).

In this sense, it is possible to recover a specific value for the social network. The participatory webs themselves can be represented as "a first space in which to articulate, in a non-individualistic sense, the presentation of the self and of relationships, in a non-instrumental sense." This relates to a peculiar space that the sociologist Ray Oldenburg has found to be well-represented in places like the cafés in the Starbucks chain: a space where one can remain alone or in company, to study or to read, in a relaxed atmosphere, in a climate of trust. This model is today being extended to social networks, which are increasingly becoming *third places*, somewhere between the public and the private, between the personal and the social: a place that allows us to put together the social puzzle, which can act as a space of intermediation, in a social context that is frayed and potentially explosive. A third place, as an environment of "relationships of experience" that allows "islands of sense" to emerge (see Oldenburg 1989; Berger and Luckmann 1967/2011).

In this sense, perhaps Dwight J. Friesen's perspective, and the perspectives of other theologians on emerging ecclesiology, can be retrieved at a pastoral level in an adequate manner, at least in their points of departure.

In the era of social networks, the Church is called to a similar task, taking on the forms that are most suitable to its mission and understanding churches also as places of significant connection for people, where it is able to furnish the basis for relationships of communion to be constructed in a fragmented society. Suggestive in this regard are the words of the theologian

Pier Angelo Sequeri (2010, 43), who has written about a new "figure of Christian settlement," which will include the "domestic, seminal, charitable and contemplative," with a view to "a new immediacy of the Christian form in the presence of God in the normal life of man." Today, a task for the Church as it is employed in the "new evangelization" could perhaps be that of creating, amongst others, spaces of connection in which people can come together to the faith and can face their most profound questions in a climate that allows the construction of relationships that are deep and in communion.

In the light of the Bible's own message, Benedict XVI (2009b) read this fundamental tension that new technologies are able to develop. This desire, he writes,

> can be read rather as a reflection of our participation in the communicative and unifying love of God, who wants to make one family from the whole of humanity. When we hear of the need to come closer to the other person, when we want to know him better and let him know us, we are responding to God's call—a call that is imprinted in our nature as beings that were created in the image and likeness of God, the God of communication and of communion.

This passage is relevant, because it connects the transformation of the Internet, understood as a "social network," to the call of God, who wants all of humanity to be one family.

More than ever, the Church finds itself being stressed by a logic of connections that, ultimately, will help her to understand more profoundly her nature as a universal instrument of *reconciliation* and *communion*. These terms are based on a radical idea of connections that today the world understands on the fly.

The sense of the Web is exactly this: the idea that we are all interconnected, each with our own roles, but that nobody can, on the other hand, put themselves ahead of somebody else to say "it has nothing to do with me." The Internet seems to be part of a whole.[15]

In these words, the conscience of the connected, global, universal person, that is the Church, can be understood to be a universal instrument that, captured in all its catholicity, finds a radical and profound harmony.

AUTHORITY, HIERARCHY, AND NETWORKS

To this same line of reflection we must add the problem of the Church's authority and of ecclesial mediation in the most general sense.[16] The first order of problems is born from the fact that, today, the Internet allows direct connection with the center of information, without any form of visible mediation. In itself, this is positive, because it allows us to obtain data, news, and comments from sources without any type of intermediate journey, and all in real time. I am thinking of the availability of the official documents of the Holy See, for example. On the other hand, the faith is not made up only of information, nor is the Church merely a place of transmission. She is not a pure "broadcaster." She is a place of witnessing, lived in the message that she proclaims: "This does not mean transmitting abstract notions, but offering an experience to be shared" (CEI 2010).

The direct relationship that is created on the Web, between the center and any point on the periphery, forms a "custom of the uselessness" of mediation incarnated in a certain moment in a certain place. The same observation, made by Lévy (1997b), who had in some ways already anticipated my thoughts in this book, applies here:

My neighbor on the landing, with whom I exchange "good day and good night," is very close to me in space, ordinary time, but is very far away from me on the plane of communication. Paradoxically, in reading a book by an author who has already been dead for three centuries, I can establish with him, in the space of signs and thought, an intellectual contact that is very strong. These people standing around me in the subway are more distant from me on the affective plane than are my daughter and my father who are five hundred kilometres away.

With the Web this fluid logic of distances is confirmed and empowered.

One can, therefore, ask oneself why one has to read a letter from one's parish priest, if one can achieve one's formation by accessing content on the Holy See website. Thanks to television, many recognize the pope's face, but do not recognize the bishop of their own diocese. However, in this recognition, how much is it the recognition of an authority, and how much, instead, is it the recognition of a celebrity?

On the other hand, Marshall McLuhan was right when, speaking of the Magisterium in the electronic era, he realized that the conditions that accompanied its exercise in the twentieth century presented an analogy with the Church's first decade. McLuhan (1999, 134) wrote:

> There is on one hand, the immediacy of the interrelation between Christians and non-Christians, in a world in which information moves at the speed of light. The population of the world now coexists in an extremely small space and in an instantaneous time. As far as this refers to the Magisterium, it is as if the whole population of the world were in a little room in which a perpetual dialogue was possible. [Thus] the Magisterium is simultaneously tried in all of the visible Church.

A second order of problems is tied to the recognition of *hierarchical* authority. Once, power and authority flowed toward a center. The Web, by its nature, is founded on links, that is, on reticular links, that are horizontal and not hierarchical: power and authority flow away from the center to the periphery. At any moment, maintains Lévy (2001, 105),

> new computers are connected, new information is put onto the Net. The more that cyberspace is extended and becomes "universal," the less the world of information adds up. The universality of cyberculture is also devoid of a centre, beyond the univocal, directing lines. It is empty, without specific content. Or, better, it wel-

comes into itself all content, because it limits itself to putting into contact any point with any other point, whatever the semantic wealth or value of the entities that are put into relationship.

Instead, the Church exists according to another logic—that of a given message, a received one, that breaks the horizontal dimension from on high. Once broken, the horizontal dimension itself lives from an authoritative witnessing, from tradition, from the magisterium, whose mission is to safeguard the people of God "from the deviations and the failures and to guarantee to them the objective possibility of professing the authentic faith without errors. The pastoral duty of the Magisterium is thus ordered to watch over the people of God so that they remain in the truth that frees them."[17] These words seem to be irreconcilable with the logic of the Web. To begin, one can say that the logic of the algorithm seems to prevail on the Web. Today, this corresponds to the Google page-ranking system, which seems to determine many people's access to knowledge. This is based on the popularity of a particular subject on Google, so what we are most likely to access are those links that are most popular. Its foundation is thus based on the knowledge that there are ways in which we agree to see things. This, for many, seems to be the best logic with which to face complexity. However, the Church cannot embrace a logic that, ultimately, is exposed to the domain that knows how to manipulate public opinion. On the Web, authority has not "disappeared," rather, it risks being even more occult.

The third and most decisive and critical moment of this general horizontality is used to dispense a transcendence, to weaken the ability to return to a reality and otherness that goes beyond us, in favor of a flattening out of immediacy and the self.

The point of reference for the symbolic dynamics that are open in the digital space is no longer a transcendent alterity, but my identity: the virtual world and an emanation of my "I"; a world that, in the end, does not explain me, does not open me to a perception of the universe and of history that is not egocentric. . . . The digital world risks, then, restructuring itself as a symbolic and auto-referential space that is closed to otherness. In the end, it is a space that is alienating: it draws me into its context until it makes itself known as a unique space of reality, even if it is not able to satisfy my search for the truth, my thirst for an understanding and a locating within a universe that goes beyond my perceptions and my thoughts. (Bressan 2010, 176)

CONTENT PASSES INTO RELATIONSHIPS

Notwithstanding the three orders of problems that are illustrated here, there is an important aspect on which to reflect: the digital society is no longer thinkable and understandable only through its contents but, above all, through its relationships and the exchange of its content, which happens within the relationships between people. The relational basis of knowledge on the Web is radical. In fact, thanks to the logic of the links, all content can be put into direct relationship with other content on the Web, wherever they are placed. Media interactivity on the Web also completes and enriches the picture. Everything that is on the Web returns to a space of connection and interaction. Web 2.0 brought this process of mobile hierarchization and of the internal knowledge of a so-called open system, to completion. It is, however, necessary not to confound this new complexity with disorder and spontaneous aggregation with anarchy.

Instead, we have to understand the Web's grammar and the articulation of authority in a fundamentally horizontal context, shared and decentralized, that calls on every individual to take up his or her responsibility and fulfill their desire for knowledge. How is this possible?

The categories and practices of witnessing are determinant. Is this a fundamental aspect? Today, the networked being trusts opinions in the form of witnessing. For example, if I want to buy a book today, or to form an opinion about it based on the opinion of others, I go to a social network like the Italian aNobii, or visit an online bookshop and read the reviews of other readers. These are more like casual observances than classic reviews; often they appeal to the personal process of reading and to the reactions that they have elicited. The same happens if I want to buy an application from the Mac App Store or a song from iTunes. Witnessing also exists on the correctness of people in the case where they are the sellers of objects on eBay. However, examples can be multiplied; they relate always to user-generated content that has had the fortune and significance to be on social networks (see Proserpio 2011). Witnessing must thus be considered inside the Web's participative logic, as user-generated content.

The witness on the Web has the traits of what de Kerckhove has defined as the "Electronic Saint." As Bertani (2007, 158) observes, these witnesses have

> an electronic aura, that is made up of all of the communicative connections that connect the person to the world and to other people. The history of the aura is very interesting, because the aura consists of its progressive disappearance; first it surrounds the entire body, then only the head, finally, it moved above the head, then it disappears. The dimension of the aura of sanctity around a holy person made up and had a therapeutic value; contact with the saint conferred health. The aura is the tactile dimension that stands between the person and the world, today it is so strong that it creates a new situation; the possibility of being tracked and traceable. We are immersed in an environment of data and information.

On the Web, the Church is thus called not only to be a broadcaster of content, but to be a "witness" in the context of broader relationships. In the words of Benedict XVI (2010): "A pastoral presence in the world of digital communications, precisely because it bings us into contact with the followers of other religions, non-believers and people of every culture, requires sensitivity to those who do not believe, the disheartened and those who have a deep, unarticulated desire for enduring truth and the absolute."

Humans today who have entered into connections that tie them to the world and other people have an "electronic aura" that makes up the shape of bearing witness in the traditional sense in the digital environment.

CHAPTER 4

Hacker Ethics and Christian Vision

The term *hacker* is part of our everyday vocabulary. Newspaper and television reports as well as films and novels have used the term in the context of code, security breaches, and the theft of personal information among other things. In the case of WikiLeaks, its founder, Julian Paul Assange, was described variously as a hacker who was attacking the world and an arsonist Web hacker, in the Italian press. In general, however, the place with which the term *hacker* commonly is associated is with experts who have managed to attack protected websites and informatics criminals.

WHO ARE THE HACKERS?

While the media have embraced this image of the hacker, the so-called information pirates really have another name: cracker. The term *hacker* singles out a person who is much more complex and constructive. "Hackers build things, the crackers break them," writes Raymond (2001), the present curator of the hacker dictionary Jargon File and the creator of the representative symbol of the hacker community. It is true that, in English, "to hack" means "to break to pieces," "to hit violently," but there is an informal use of the term that means "to deal with," "to put up with." Hackers are therefore people who employ themselves in confronting intellectual challenges so as to bypass or creatively overcome the limitations that are imposed on them in their own areas of interest. Furthermore, the term refers to experts in informatics, but it can itself be extended to people who live many other aspects of their lives in a creative manner. To be a hacker is, in short, a philosophy of life, an attitude that pushes creativity and sharing, opposing models of control and competition, and private ownership. One senses, therefore, that speaking in the actual way of a hacker, one finds oneself not confronted with a problem of a criminal order, but with a vision of human work, knowledge, and life. This raises timely questions.

In his book, *Hackers*, the technologist Stephen Levy (2002) presented what he judged to be the "seven commandments; of the personal computer revolution." These have since been the basis of the so-called hacker ethics:

1. Access to computers must be unlimited and total.
2. Always give priority to the hands-on, and to personally check.
3. All information must be free.
4. Distrust authority, promoting decentralization.
5. Hackers must be judged by their hacking.
6. It is possible to create art and beauty on a computer.
7. Computers can change your life for the better.

In this list, we find a clear synthesis that speaks of freedom of action, of the importance of experimentation and verification, of the distrust of any form of authority, and of a fundamental optimism about the human capacity.

Levy lists a series of attitudes that had matured many years previously, at the end of the 1960s and in the 1970s, when a generation of young people who were passionate about the computer had emerged in the San Francisco Bay Area. They were united by their interest in spreading the use of those machines even beyond the restricted academic environment, convinced that this could improve people's lives. The first project for the spread and social use of informatics began in 1969 when the Community Memory at Berkeley was founded. Community Memory was formed to put together a data bank linked to the city in such a way that—through terminals set up in places like laundromats, libraries, and shops—the exchange of information and opinions would be possible amongst its inhabitants.

To help improve the actual computer infrastructure so that it would be possible to spread these new machines amongst the population, the Homebrew Computer Club was born. This was an association of engineers, researchers, and technicians who shared the dream of popularizing informatics and to construct a new and revolutionary prototype computer. In 1976 Steve Wozniak, a twenty-five-year-old member of the club, built the Apple I, the first personal computer that was accessible even to ordinary people.

THE PLAYFUL EFFORT OF CREATION

Another member of the Homebrew Computer Club was Tom Pittman, one of the first philosopher hackers. In his manifesto, *Deus ex Machina, or the true computerist,* he tried to promulgate the idea of the sensation that might accompany the real hacker in this creative process. "I, who am a Christian, felt able to come close to that type of satisfaction that God may have felt when he created the world" (Himanen 2001, 141). In effect, the hacker has a precise perception of the importance of giving a personal and original contribution to knowledge. Pittman (2008), who presents himself as a Christian and a technologist, interprets this action as emotive participation in the creative work of God, a work that develops interests, passions, and curiosity and sets the capacity of those who do it in motion, without demeaning it. Substantially, the hacker is a creative person who is always doing research. As a Christian, he lives and interprets his creative gesture as a form of participation in God's "work" of creation.

Applied creativity is one of the salient points of the hacker spirit. Raymond (2001) writes, "the world is full of fascinating problems that wait to be resolved." The hacker employs himself with the happy spirit and strong motivation to exercise his own intelligence to resolve problems. In this sense, there is a rejection of work that is "repetitive, hard and stupid." The hacker is capable of great achievements because he is strongly motivated. This does not at all exclude commitment and it abhors idleness, but he feels that its difficulty is gladdened by creative motivation.

Pekka Himanen (2001), lecturer at the University of Helsinki and the University of California at Berkeley, began from these presuppositions and developed a reflection that had nothing directly to do with theology when he wrote *The Hacker Ethic and the Spirit of the Age of Information*. In particular, he articulates a profound critique of the protestant ethic approach, understood in Max Weber's (2002) capitalist sense, which imposes what he defines as the "Fridayisation of Sunday." Its thrust is directed against a certain understanding of the existence of the whole unbalanced workflow, which is tied to the clock and to performance and efficiency. Himanen (2001, 32) proposes, alternatively, a vision of human work that is more playful and creative, a "Saturdayisation of Friday." Himanen puts us on our guard against the Fordist scheme of production, which molds our ordinary life in favor of a new work ethic that is characterized by passion and creativity and not limited by shifts and rigid times, and without the capacity to save. Under accusation are control, competition, and ownership. It is a vision that, rather than being idealized, clearly has a theological origin. His basic question is, in fact, the "direction of life," as an important paragraph in his book tells us: "One can say that the original response of Christianity to the question: 'What is the direction of life?' would be 'The direction of life is Sunday'" (13). His references are Dante's *Divine Comedy*, "the apotheosis of the vision of the pre-protestant world" (15), and *Agostino e la Navigatio Sancti Brendani*, an anonymous work in Latin prose, that has been handed down through numerous manuscripts since the tenth century. Reflecting on Augustine, who wrote on Genesis against the Manicheans, Himanen notes that for the Saint of Hippo, "living in Eden was more honourable than hard" (14). For the sinners in Dante's hell, instead, "Sunday is always something tempting, but it never arrives. They are condemned to an eternal Friday." The Reformation, in his judgment, has moved the center of life's gravity from Sunday to Friday, and at this point it became difficult to imagine Paradise as a place of simple fun. While, in visionary mediaeval representations, sinners were punished with hammers and instruments of work, the reformed pastor of the eighteenth century, Johann Kasper Lavater, was able to write that "we cannot be blessed without having an occupation" (16). It is this vision of blessedness that comes from work that constitutes the ideological basis of a novel like Daniel Defoe's *Robinson Crusoe* (1719).

The hacker ethic wants to overturn the protestant ethic, affirming that the direction of life is nearer to Sunday than to Friday. It is not difficult to recognize the intuition of a "blessed life" in the genetic code of the hacker vision of life; the intuition of the human being is called to another life, to a full realization accomplished by his own humanity. Obviously, the hacker is not an idle man or woman, of "dolce far niente" (it is sweet to do nothing). On the contrary, hackers are very active. They follow their own passions and lives driven by a creative force and knowledge that is never ending. However, they know that their humanity is not realized through a rigidly organized schedule, but through the flexible rhythm of a creativity that must become the measure of truly human work, which better corresponds to man's nature.

Closely connected to the Sunday tension of the hacker ethic is mistrust of the principle of authority. One of the key points of the hacker vision of human action consists in not referring to an authority to whom one owes obedience. As I have noted in regard to Stephen Levy's decalogue, this is founded on decentralization, comes from a decentralized authority, and is playful and creative. With the rise of social networks, today this vision is becoming a mentality. The idea is thus spreading that wide-ranging sharing is an important route to the production and diffusion of ideas and knowledge. The success of the "ecosystem" that is Web 2.0 is changing our productive and social panorama.

In particular, the Web involves connections to resources, time, and ideas about sharing *generously*. The classic example is that of Wikipedia. Compiling this major collaborative encyclopaedia of the Web took an estimated one hundred million hours of intellectual work, which is about as much time as the citizens of the United States combined spend watching advertising on television in a weekend. Wikipedia is the result of the free convergence of competences, ideas, free time, and the critical capacity of many people on the planet who are connected amongst themselves (Lih 2009). This is a good response to the criteria of hacker ethics: flexible and creative *work* based on the sharing of passions and interests, which in turn has evoked a sense of Utopia that has always guided the evolution of Wikipedia. Obviously, Utopia has made us consider original sin, that is, imprecisions and errors, in search of a redemption that the system cannot itself give. However, notwithstanding its limits, Wikipedia has signaled a net change: while the traditional media (including books and traditional encyclopaedias) substantially permitted consumption of what was *produced*, the Internet allowed us to be able to imagine, for example, free time as a shared global resource, and we can imagine new types of participation. In this regard, Clay Shirky (2010) reflected on this type of "cognitive surplus," as the title of one of his celebrated books suggested. In his view, this surplus is being characterized as an emerging and vital force, able to gather a delocalized and fragmented knowledge and to aggregate it into something new. This sharing does not answer to any center, or to any authority. It is a sort of biological process of growth and extension.

The intellectually collaborative organization that emerges on the Web, with its great cognitive surplus, can therefore allow the same idea of cultural production to change. It is a clear outcome of the hacker philosophy, an effect of sorts on a popular and planetary scale of its assumptions. Obviously, it is an optimistic vision that sees only the good in this evolutionary process. We need to ask ourselves better questions about the problems of the management of this surplus value that is created, perhaps always remembering that the "original sin" of Wikipedia is all one with its intrinsic and innovative qualities. Pierre Lévy (2001, 11) was right to put us on guard against the weaknesses and problems of interactive digital networks, where we can also see new forms of isolation and of cognitive superwork, prevarication, control, exploitation, and collective stupidity springing up. In reality, many questions are emerging: What will society do with all of this surplus value? How can a new, quality idea arise? Do we have the right motivations, beyond the opportunities, to do something with them? The possible distortions are clear as well: the traditional organizational forms are being threatened, diminishing the power of institutions and, in the end, taking the power from society to act, for example, as a contrast, to deviant group behaviors.

In particular, what both collaborative and hacker knowledge seem to obscure is the principle of authority, as Stephen Levy's fourth commandment states. This creates a precise mentality in a way that confronts the experience of living relationships and of knowing reality.

How can we put a value on this mentality? If it is interesting to confront the argument, it is because the model of knowledge, as the fruit of horizontal sharing and not of a hierarchy, is already a given in the lives of many people. I have mentioned this previously in reference to Wikipedia, but already this has become a classic icon of a broader movement, of a mindset that touches many worlds, including the worlds of journalism, education, and research.[1]

Above all, it is important not to canonize the hacker's needs, that is, not to consider them as though they had no history, since development also has a significance that is tied to a historical period. The origin of hacker culture dates back to the end of the 1960s in the United States, a period that was characterized by the anarchy of the hippy movement and a radical critique of the "system" and of the values that were dominant at the time. The hacker ethic, then, risks expressing needs that are born from an impatience with any form of hierarchy, because it was understood as being necessarily opposed to research and comparison. There is a rejection of the "father" in favor of horizontal dealings amd joint collaborations. In the general valuation of that culture, this element of sociological order, which, in a way, can therefore be considered dated.

On the other hand, it is true that a precise research model is emerging, one that goes beyond the historic moment in which it was born. In one of his celebrated stories, entitled "The Cathedral and the Bazaar," Raymond (2010) counterposes two models of research: the bazaar and the cathedral. Once again, a religious metaphor has emerged, and the reasoning has theological resonance. It is necessary to clarify the two models that have a theological appeal. Raymond's primary intent is to describe a new model of software development. In effect, his text generally is considered the movement's open source manifesto. This type of software is considered *open* because its developers favor free study and the inclusion of modifications that come from other independent programmers. Its source code is open to free and spontaneous collaboration. Open source therefore describes a model of free work, open to collaborations that are not restrained by private ownership. Linux is an operating system that applies this associated model of development. Raymond's story thus distinguished two models of research. The first is that of the cathedral, in which the program is realized by a limited number of experts on the basis of a hierarchical subdivision. The second is that of the bazaar, in which the open source program being developed is freely available. Development is thus decentralized and no rigid subdivision of tasks exists. This is a process of sharing in which participants contribute to the improvement of the program, which continues in small steps toward ever new and better versions. The cathedral becomes a metaphor of a system with clear, defined, and hierarchical roles. The bazaar, by contrast, is a metaphor for the open system.

Pekka Himanen (2001, 63–81) takes up this notion of the cathedral and the bazaar in a more classic manner, using the metaphors of academia and of the monastery. Once again, there is a clear religious metaphor. The academic model comes from platonic origins and is based on collective research, which in turn is based on exchange and self-regulation. In the platonic academy, in fact, drawing closer to the truth was sought through critical dialogue and the free circulation of results. "Students were not considered objectives for the transmission of knowledge, but companions in learning (synthesis). In academic conceptions, the principal task of teaching was that of reinforcing the ability of disciples to pose problems, in developing lines of thought and in advancing critiques" (75). Instead, the monastic model would be a closed, hierarchical model into which only a limited group of people was welcomed and the objective of study was established once and for all. From this it can be seen that the cathedral and the monastery single out places from which to flee in favor of the bazaar and academia.

Himanen crystallizes the image of the monastery so as to bend it into a negative icon. This is his principal limitation. We know well that a partial reading of monastic mediaeval life deems it to have been signalled by sociological flattening out, thus killing its significance. It would be rather reductive to consider the cathedral and the monastery models in the sense in which Raymond and Himanen understand them, as though they were ecclesiological models.

REVELATION IN THE BAZAAR

Today, the academic model has become popular, especially with the birth of Wikipedia. In confronting this form of collective knowledge on the Web, the stress has been strong. Justin Baeder, the creator of Radical Congruency, asked: "What implications can these Websites have for the Church? What implications can they have for a communitarian approach to theology?"[2]

With these questions, Baeder's intentions do not solely relate to pastoral applications. He intends to ask whether wikis can inspire a way of doing theology, can become a type of theological method. He responds to the question by indicating so-called "open source theology." The expression uses informatics jargon, referring to the open source license, in which, as we have seen, the open source program is made available to developers, so that with their collaboration (which is, in general, free and spontaneous) the final product can reach a greater complexity than it would have from the work of a single group of programmers.

By contrast, Andrew Perriman uses "open source theology" to indicate a way of doing theology that is "exploratory, open to conclusions, incomplete, less preoccupied with establishing fixed points and boundaries than with nourishing a dialogue that both reminds us of and is constructive between, text and context."[3] It is important to note that this method of *collaborative theology*, as it has also been defined, attributes to theological reflection, which is understood not as pure academic study but as a communitarian activity that is dynamically developed inside precise historical contexts.

However, the serious case here is the following: what is the open source of theology? Or Revelation? What is left *open* in the most disparate forms of reading: applications and presentations. Open source theology is very ambiguous because it clearly cedes the risk of a flattening out of sociological order, or it is vaguely humanistic. Is it a loss or misunderstanding of the *depositum fide?* In fact, if the open source of theology, Revelation, does not solely become elaborated at the level of the *interface*—that is, at the level of categories of comprehension and communication—but is also modified in itself, then we will no longer be before a Christian theology, but of a more general discussion on themes with theological-religious significance. Add to this a vagueness, the rejection of any form of authoritative charisma and a disinterest in traditions, considered an "imperial" form, as Brian McLaren has defined them.[4] Christianity will tend to assume the characteristics of a "participative narration," realized by individuals or groups within frames and contexts that are culturally disparate.

At this point, one should ask: Would the hacker ethic not be on a collision course with the Catholic mind and its vision of authority and tradition? Would it be possible to encompass authority, in the sense in which Catholic theology understands it, in a context that pushes toward decentralization and to the dehierarchization of knowledge? Intrinsically, collective action and the principle of authority are in radical opposition; how would this be taken for granted? The panorama described would, to this point, certainly cause us to confront a *forma mentis* with which the Catholic faith must develop an ever greater relationship. This calls for a new form of apologetics, which cannot but begin from the changed categories of comprehension of the world and of access to knowledge.

Tom Pittman has expressed himself often on the illogicality of atheism and has professed himself to be a Christian, yet other experiences also demonstrate that between the faith and the hacker it is possible to create syntony. For example, the programming language Perl (which stands for Practical Extraction and Report Language) was originally called Pearl, in reference to the "Pearl of Great Price" (Matthew 13.46), which causes a merchant to sell all he has in order to buy it. It was created in 1987 by the hacker Larry Wall, who is an evangelical Christian. Besides giving such names as "bless," "apocalypse," and "exegesis" to functions in his language, often, when speaking at conferences and congresses, Wall makes reference to his Christian faith. Like Pittman and others, he strongly joins his creative action to his own faith: "Perl is obviously my attempt to help others to be creative. Humbly, I am helping people to have a little more understanding about who are the people who please God, who is the absolute model, the 'cosmic artist'?" (Roblimo 2002). In this vision, the hacker ethic can even take on prophetic resonances for the world of today, which has chosen the logic of profit, to remember that the "human heart longs for a world in which love reigns and where gifts are shared" (Benedict XVI 2009b).

THE GIFT OF THE WEB:
PEER-TO-PEER OR FACE TO FACE?

It is well understood that one of the critical points for reflection on what is on the Web that goes under the term *open* is, in reality, the concept of the *gift*, made even more radical by free software or freeware. The Web is the place of the gift. Concepts like file sharing, free software, open source, creative commons, user-generated content, social networks, all have within them, even if in a different way, the concept of the gift, of the abatement of the idea of profit (Aime and Cossetta 2011). If well considered, however, this is a *free exchange* that is made possible and significant thanks to a form of reciprocity, *profitable* for those who participate in this exchange. There is the *economic* idea that has in its mind the concept of the market, and even a business model.[5]

The Web molds a mentality of sharing that is substantially one of exchange. One of the critical points of the hacker vision is open source, and thus that of the intrinsic limits to every sharing: scarcity. It is true that the hacker culture is a gift culture, but here the gift assumes a free form. Its thrust is not to give and receive, but to take and leave what the others take. Reduction to the gift is something that is a given of the object in itself, risking the obscuring of the perception of a deeper dynamic, of which the gesture of giving is the expression (Mancini 2011, 41–46). With the concept of the gift, the concept of the neighbor changes as well. For the single subject, the receiver, the user is substituted. Under this condition, the donor does not offer an object that in some way represents the relationship between him and the receiver. The donor offers something that is not signaled by a unique affective relationship. On the other hand, he does not even know the receiver: we could say that he gives the gift to society (Aime 2002; Mauss 1990). The model of the Web that most radically reflects this dimension of gift exchange is that of equals, which is called *peer-to-peer* (P2P). This model does not have any hierarchical nodes, like fixed clients and servers, but a number of equivalent nodes that are open to other nodes on the Web and can receive and transmit at the same time. When I initiate a download on a P2P network, my computer takes *bits* (videos, music, texts) from many individual computers that are contemporaneously connected on the Web and that contain that document. In its turn, my computer, while it is downloading, permits other computers to load bits of that file, or of other files that I make available. In the end, all will be reassembled on a single computer. The process is called *file sharing* and is therefore characterized as sharing. This technology easily permits the downloading of multimedia files, even the largest ones, within a reasonable period of time, or to find a multiplicity of rare materials. The motive for this technology has often been contested because it permits the downloading of anything without cost, violating prerogative copyrights.

In other words, peer-to-peer logic is thus based on the fact that I download something in its entirety, but not from a unique repository that contains it whole, or in a one-to-one relationship. I share what I have at the same moment that I receive it. However, I never receive content in its entirety. I receive in a process that makes me also a node in a shared network of exchange and I am, at that moment, "rich" since I can now give to others what I have so far received. If this is applied at the ethical level of the distribution of goods, this logic of sharing appears to be without problems and, rather, to be decidedly virtuous.[6] In some ways, it comes close to blood donation, which represents a form of gift addressed to unknown people. These people are determined by peculiar characteristics that differentiate them from the traditional Maussian gift (Mauss 1990), which implicates not only the giving but also the receiving and the returning. Neither restitution nor obligation are foreseen; the same object of the altruistic act of blood donation always consists of the same substance: blood, which can be received and given in a vision of the symbolic restitution inside a temporal dimension. This also is symbolic with regard to the perception of the diachronic nearness or farness of the gift received. If we apply this logic to the theological level, however, we understand that the question becomes more problematic just because of the Church's nature and the dynamics of Christian Revelation, which seem to follow a client-server model that is the opposite of peer-to-peer.

These are not the product of a horizontal exchange (which we can define more correctly as "fluid barter"), but are the opening to a deductible and inexhaustible grace that passes through traditions and hierarchical, sacramental, and historical mediation. If we stop here, we risk reaching a radical incompatibility between the logic of theology and that of the Web.

In reality, the question is more complicated. The logic of the gift on the Web seems to be tied to what is called in slang a *freebie*, that is, something that has no price, in the sense that it costs nothing. This is founded on the implicit question, "what does it cost?"; and the vision is all displaced onto who *takes* (and not on who *receives*). The freebie is something (on the Web it is generally a program or digital content) that one can take freely. Another version of exchange that follows this logic is what is tied to the freemium: something that can be retrieved or downloaded, for example, a free or trial version of a program that requires payment to unlock its full feature set. The principle on which this model is founded is the business freemium, which is given when it is convenient to gift something to users with the intention of selling them products or services at a more advanced level. In short, one can speak of the "price" of the "freeness" (Anderson 2009).

THE FREELY GIVEN GIFT

Gratia gratis data, as it is theologically understood, means that one does not *take* but receives, and one always enters into a relationship beyond which we have no understanding. Grace is not a freebie but rather, to quote Bonhoeffer, it has been paid for "at a high price," and without limitations, and its freeness does not answer to the logic of profit. At the same time, grace is communicated through incarnate mediation and is spread through capillaries in a logic that is compatible with that of peer-to-peer networking, but is not reducible to it. In fact, it can be anonymous, on an individual basis, and impersonal: one can take all that is available, and one doesn't know how much of the actual files will be shared.

The logic of grace creates *ties*, face to face, as is typical of the logic of the gift, of communicating faces, a thing that is instead extraneous per se of peer-to-peer logic, which is a logic of connections and exchange, of communicating vessels, not of communion. A face is never reducible to a simple *node*. The true gift has in itself, at least in an implicit way, the potential to create relationships, contrary to the pure market that generates exchange. The gift is a gesture that gains significance within an experience of relationship. Obviously, part of the anonymous peer-to-peer file sharing is the logic of the user-generated content of social networks. Formally, the second appears to be more compatible with a theological logic, because the shared content is *given* within a relationship and as recompense it has the relationship itself, that is, the increment and improvement of reciprocal relationships.

This, as I have said, does not signify in itself that peer-to-peer logic is mistaken or negative. On the contrary, it is significant in the context of general and broad sharing. It is, though, important to understand that the theological logic of the gift is not reducible to this, that, or the other. The logic of the gift that is being developed on the Internet leads us to sharing, solidarity, and cooperation, in which generosity can remain anonymous, as has been demonstrated in the innovative processes of free software.[7] It is the logic of the gift as grace that insists on personal relationships, which it is not possible to leave aside. However, it is actually on this difference that the challenge for believers is founded: from a place of connections, the Web is called to become, as I have said, a place of communion. Only if giving corresponds to receiving, alerting us also to the gratitude that pushes toward recompense (Mauss 1990, 10–23), is it possible to create relationships that are not extraneous to involvement.

The risk of these times is to confound the two terms: connection does not automatically produce a communion; it is also a *conditio sine qua non.* The connection itself is not enough to make the Web a place where sharing is fully human. It is true that connections create communities, but they are not essential to the actual relations, ties, familiarity, and their consequences (see Bauman 2001). The new communities risk considering physicality to be an accessory, as well as all of the baggage that is tied to the language that is incarnated in the body. Relationships end up by being substantially founded on rhetorical practices, and this would be a gross impoverishment, the key word is thus *integration*; between the different levels of the lived.

By contrast, if the "human heart longs for a world in which love reigns, where gifts are shared," as Benedict XVI (2009b) has written, then the Web can truly be a privileged environment in which this profoundly human need can take shape. This is, in fact, the most significant and virtuous aspect of the free, as it is understood on the Web: the fact that the *gifts* are open to the practices of sharing beause they are available, free. Above all, this appears to be evident when we speak of the production of cultural value. When an environment that facilitates collaboration among people is cultivated, a context of creativity and generosity that multiplies the forces and results is created. The wiring of humanity (or at least of that part of it that is effectively joined to the Web) permits the sharing of resources in a global way, and the imagining of new forms of participation and sharing (Shirky 2010, 22).

This anonymous collaboration is a social production, and a commons-based peer production, that is, a work of production created by people who operate on the same level, based on collective, accessible goods, on the part of its participants.[8] To define the gift in this way is not communion, but one of the ways in which we can understand solidarity today, or all of the forms of gift that do not imply a face-to-face relationship.

THE SURPLUS OF GRACE
AND THE COGNITIVE SURPLUS

Christian Revelation, "by means of which God turned and gave himself to man" (Catechism 1993, no. 14), is instead a gift deductible from collaborative exchange of a horizontal type. Theologically understood, the freeness of grace does not respond to the logic of profit. This is certainly communicated through incarnate mediation and is spread through capillaries, but is not reducible to a logic of connections, which can be very anonymous, and on an individual and impersonal basis. The risk of a hacker-type state of mind is thus that of leading us to understand communion as a connection, and the gift as free exchange. The order of knowledge of Revelation is peculiar in this: "Man cannot possibly arrive on his own." It is instead "by a wholly free decision" that "God reveals himself and gives himself to man, revealing his mystery" (no. 50).

Ecclesiology, in its turn, is not reducible to the sociology of ecclesial relationships: "The Church is in history, but at the same time it transcends it. It is uniquely 'with the eyes of faith' that one can make out a contemporary spiritual reality, the carrier of divine life, in its visible reality" (no. 770). The Church is founded, then, not on a collaborative process, but on the "foundation of the Apostles" (Ephesians 2.20), witnesses who were chosen and sent on the mission by Christ himself. She "houses and transmits with the help of the Spirit who lives there, the teaching, the good deposit, the healthy words heard by the Apostle" (no. 857). In short, in the challenge that the hacker mentality begins to put on theology and the faith—that is, preserving human openness to transcendence—is a nondeductible gift to a grace that breaks the system of relationships and is never only the fruit of a connection, nor of a sharing, as much as it is broad and generous. A principle of *auctoritas sano* will be preserved that enhances the foundation, external to man and to his possibilities for Revelation and grace. In brief, we must remind ourselves that life and its significance are not exhaustible in a horizontal Web, but that humans are always oriented to transcendence. In the final analysis, the problem of authority is a form of the more general problem of the possibility of transcendence. In this context, we should note something that is more important than ever: the distinction between knowledge and wisdom, between notions and values. The Church is not, and will never be, simply a cognitive society, and the logic of grace is different from that of information. These are the reflections that the Catholic vision of authority turns to in a critical manner in the hacker culture.

With the abolition of any hierarchy, we will lose the importance of mediations and of the pedagogic dimensions of access to knowledge. According to this logic, neither past nor knowledge is handed down from father to son, because the principle of sameness, of perfect symmetry, is in force. However, we must confirm that the hacker community is not monolithic and that its anti-authoritarian being does not lead it to negate any type of authority. Raymond (2001) writes that anti-authoritarianism "does not signify fighting all of the authorities. Children must be guided and criminals corrected. A hacker can be in agreement with accepting some type of authority." Governance, with hacker inspiration, can help us to better understand the presuppositions and effects of a form of "distributed authority."[9] In a critical manner, seriously and without complacency, the hacker spirit can help us to understand that the transcendent foundation of the faith sets an open process in motion, which is creative, collaborative, and collegial. Raymond reminds us that the basis of the sharing of the hacker spirit is founded on a moral duty: to ensure that common work problems are resolved more easily and rapidly. This solidarity lives from a relationship of community between people who are ready to help themselves and to collaborate. Further, the call to creativity can help us to understand how "the Spirit builds soul and sanctifies the Church" living in its live body (Compendium, no. 145), animating it from within. In an ecclesial context, we realize what Shirky (2010) called the "surplus." However, this is not only immanent, the fruit of the efforts of believers, it is a sanctifying surplus that comes from the action of the Spirit, who enlivens the members of the mystic body. Christ, in fact, "has participated His Spirit that, one and the same in head and limbs, gives life to, unifies and energizes the entire body" (Paul VI 1964). The dynamic element of the Church, which makes it much more than the simple sum of its parts, is just that Holy Spirit. In hacker theory, there is at least a specific place in which the transcendent dimensions can cosily express themselves, and this is in the radical call to the fact that Shabbat, Saturday (Sunday, in Christian terms), is the real "homeland" of humans, our true existential dimension. The Jewish Saturday, or the Christian Sunday, can obviously not just be reduced to rest.

However, the hacker Sunday is not even a simple "holiday" in which, at least implicitly, a reference to God lives, in as much as He is the creative origin of the world. The creation is able to give to the hacker vision of the world, and of humans, that "point of departure" that is transcendent, without there being a risk of finishing in an alley that is colorful, but blind.

Himanen (2001), the self-proclaimed popularizer of the hacker ethic, remembers that "in one of his two Apologetics in favour of the Christianity of the second century, one of the Fathers of the Church, Justin the Martyr, eulogises Sunday" (149). He cites his source: "We all gather together on the day of the Sun, because this is the first day in which God, having transformed the shades and matter, created the world. On this day also, Jesus Christ, our Saviour, was resurrected from the dead" (149). At this point, Himanen poses the question which we find in St. Augustine, "Why did God create the world?"; he continues: "We can say that the hackers reply to Augustine's question is that God, as he is perfect, *had no need* to make absolutely anything, but wanted to create" (152). In the story of the free and removeable creative actions of God, the hacker finds the image of his own existence.

> Genesis can be seen as a story about a mode of creative activity. In this, talents are used in an imaginative way. It reflects on the joy that you feel when you begin to surprise yourself by outdoing yourself. Not a day passes when God is not present with an idea that is even more extraordinary: like actualizing hairless, bipedal creatures. He is so excited at having created a world made for others that he is even ready to stay awake for six nights in a row, resting a little only on the seventh day. (152)

If this biblical model is removed from its profoundly theological value, then it is able to maintain the memory of an initiative that is the fruit of a creative act of God.

CHAPTER 5

Liturgy, Sacraments, and Virtual Presence

At the beginning of the 1970s, the great mass media scholar Marshall McLuhan and his son Eric hypothesized on the destiny of religion in the West under the influence of the electronic media (McLuhan 1999, ch. 7; see also Baragli 1974, 195–210). Today, this question seems to gain in significance thanks to the capillary diffusion of the digital media and of the technologies of the Web. Are the Internet and the digital media perhaps changing the way we live and understand the liturgy? Is it possible to imagine a form of liturgy and the sacraments on the Web? The questions are complex and must be articulated and understood well to avoid misunderstandings and too facile conclusions. The first level of the questions has its roots in years of transmission of Eucharistic celebrations on television. Today, this tradition has the potential to expand even further thanks to the Web.

FROM THE MICROPHONE ON
THE ALTAR TO THE AVATAR'S PRAYER

First, I would like to set the context for the problematic that we are facing today: the introduction of the microphone into liturgical contexts. The attention used to be given to the environment created by the liturgy, in a context made up of sounds, colors, scents, orientation, objects, and movements. The words of the priest became part of the context, because his voice could not be heard equally well throughout the congregation. With the advent of the microphone and its presence on the altar, the congregation entered into an immediate relationship with the speaker, with the celebrant, who could turn to them directly and speak clearly and loudly. In terms of the use of the microphone, McLuhan had thus synthesized the change. We can observe in the liturgy that the acoustic amplification overloads our auditory sensorial channels, lowering the threshold of attention to the visual and individual experience of the liturgy so that it isolates the individual in a sound bubble within the architectural space (McLuhan 1999, 110).

McLuhan argues that the amplified voice (in the vernacular) created a direct relationship between the celebrant and the individual, between the center and a point in the congregation, where previously the voice was not amplified and was also, in fact, in Latin, creating a "corporate distance."

However, it is also true that the microphone creates a type of sound cloud that surrounds all of the participants; a spherical cloud in which the center is everywhere and the circumference is nowhere. Without the microphone, the orator is only a unique center while, with the microphone, he is everywhere at the same time (ibid.).

The questions that digital culture and life pose for the liturgy can already be traced in the changes that ensued when, for the first time, the microphone was placed on an altar. That "spherical cloud without circumference and with an ubiquitous center," of which McLuhan spoke, has today expanded—thanks to the medium of radio, digital technologies, and the Web—from the perimeter of a church to the whole world. Today, if a priest speaks into a microphone, his voice and his picture can, through audio/video streaming, reach anyone, anywhere in the world as long as an Internet connection is available.

However, the reality is still more complex. If we think of simulated worlds like that in the virtual world game *Second Life* (Spadaro 2007; Leone 2010), it seems that, with the growth of virtual spaces, an increasing number of people feel the need to create places of prayer—or even churches, cathedrals, cloisters, and convents—to take a break and meditate. The list of the churches on *Second Life* is long: there are cathedrals, like the simulations of the Catholic Notre Dame in Paris and Salzburg Cathedral, and basilicas like St. Francis in Assisi. There is also an Anglican cathedral, where liturgical services are held at set hours, and other initiatives like the Church of Fools.[1] We can enter this world thanks to its own virtual representation, to its own virtual ego, which in jargon is defined as an *avatar*. Can an avatar participate in a prayer event?[2] Is it possible that an avatar can live a form of communal prayer that can be considered liturgical? Is it possible to think of a virtual Eucharistic celebration where avatars receive the Eucharistic species in the simulated world? Paul S. Fiddes, Baptist minister and professor of systematic theology at Oxford, takes this up in a brief text that was circulated on the Web, provoking a wide debate.[3]

ARE THERE SACRAMENTS ON THE INTERNET?

The first observation to make is that the question has taken off due to concrete experiences and not just from abstract speculation on the things that are possible: there are realities on the Web that define themselves as liturgical. Perhaps one of the first was in 1997, when Stephen C. Rose began to put the text of a "Cyber-Eucharist" online.[4] The person who participated in the liturgy had to sit down in front of a computer, with bread and wine within reach, and read the text aloud. This was obviously something that was completely extraneous to what we understand as liturgy; it had none of the elements of this experience and did not foresee even a minimal type of interactivity and sharing. It is not surprising, therefore, that the experiment lasted only for a very short time.

Reverend Tim Ross, an English Methodist minister, had imagined a communion service would be possible on Twitter.[5] The celebration has never happened because the authorities of his ecclesiastical community asked him to cancel it, while considering the motivation that had caused the Reverend Ross to think of it to be valid, that is, as a "renewed expression of faith and worship in the context of new forms of electronic social media."[6] The celebration was thought of as a remote communion, which happens when those who receive the Eucharistic species take them at the same moment, but not in the same physical space as the celebrant, as Reverend Ross explained.[7] Reverend Ross also cited the case of a parish in the Church of Scotland that put celebrations online in order to gather the faithful, who were spread across various small islands and who would otherwise not have any way of coming together.[8] He affirmed that to consider the celebration valid, it was necessary to consider "remote communion" valid or, rather, in addition to consider the Christian community that meets on the Web, trusting in what Jesus had said—"where two or three are gathered together in my name, I am in the midst of them" (Matthew 18.20)—without further specifications. In fact, Ross believes, it is the presence of God that makes a group of people a community, and not their spatial proximity. In this mode, the sense of community given by social networks will be superimposed (with the risk of coinciding) on that of the ecclesial community.

The Catholic Church always insists that it is impossible and anthropologically erroneous to consider virtual reality to be *able* to substitute for the real, tangible, and concrete experience of the

Christian community: the same applies, visibly and historically, to liturgical celebrations and sacraments. By virtual reality, we understand a multimedia, interactive experience undertaken by a means of communication connected to the Web (Heim 1998, 3). The document *The Church and the Internet* (2002), published by the Pontifical Council for Social Communication, was very clear in this regard: virtual reality cannot substitute for the real presence of Christ in the Eucharist, the sacramental reality of the other sacraments and worship at which we participate in the heart of a human community, in body and blood. There are no sacraments on the Internet. Even the religious experiences that are possible through the grace of God are insufficient if separated from interaction with the real world and with the other faithful (no. 9).

The response is clear in repairing any drift that abstracts the sacramental dimension from what is incarnate in visible and tangible signs. For the rest, in a strict sense, the concept of the *virtual sacraments* is founded on the fact that it would be an avatar that would receive God's grace, which, from this avatar, would be transferred to the person of whom that avatar is an extension. Behind this thought process is the reductive idea that to receive a sacrament in substance signifies simply being involved in a psychological way in an event, whether real or virtual. Pathos takes the place of Logos. In this sense, bread and wine, like water in the case of baptism, would all be accessory elements and, in the end, without any real relevance. Following on this trajectory, the imagination that is activated in this context tends to translate into "simulation" or "consensual hallucination" (Gibson 1984) which causes the believer to identify him- or herself in the situation or way in which he/she wants to live.

There is, instead, still a possibility that is open for digital devotion that can in some way be tied to various forms of spiritual communion, which has always been noted in the traditions, as the Council of Trent attested,[9] and the same document, *The*

Church and the Internet, speaks of "religious experiences that are possible by the grace of God," even on the Web.

IS NETWORKING AN EXPERIENCE OF COMMUNION?

Surrounding the experience of communion that is realized through social networks, connected to possible Eucharistic celebrations online, is a need to understand how this experience can be a critical point. The Church cannot be reduced to the "ultimate social network," a sort of definitive social web, because it is not just a web of immanent relationships. Yet, this image of the social web is increasingly molding believers' imaginations. It is enough to think, for example, of the experiment of sharing our own experience of God during Easter via Twitter, even while in church.[10] If this sharing happens at a suitable moment—such as participation, when it has personal resonance—the proposal would be very interesting, but the experiment to which I am referring does not foresee remote communion; it presents an ambiguity that is unresolvable if it is lived during *live* celebrations, because there is a risk of alienation. If we share our own experience with others who are absent, we will end up neglecting what we are living with the faithful who are present. The sense of participation—as *taking part* in a celebration that is absolutely not reducible to its psychological components or to the stimulation into which the sense of participating in a video game is transformed (see Highland and Yu 2008)—must also be discussed.

The fundamental risk that seems joined to the experience of the liturgy on the Web is that of a flow of "magic" that is able to fade away, until the sense of community and ecclesial mediation that is incarnated is canceled, so as to exalt instead the role of the technology that makes the event possible. What is the difference between a live concert followed online thanks to technology—which allows us an immersive experience (fast connections, good domestic audio equipment and so on)—and a liturgical celebration? Here, it is clear that the broadest questions in regard to sacred liturgies and profane liturgies (which are those that are celebrated in stadia, big shows, or concerts) begin to emerge. However, the level of reflection that the Web requires for the role of the technology that makes the virtual presence possible in a context like ours, where the media have been let loose in the ordinary environment in which we live, must go further. Underneath, the "magic" functions of the Web actually consist of the negation of spatial distance, of allowing us to "grab" what is far away, to establish direct and efficacious contact with what is beyond our control, which is distant in many ways.

THE LITURGY AND ITS
TECHNOLOGICAL REPRODUCTION

The question of liturgy on the Web is perhaps similar to that posed in 1936 by Walter Benjamin about the work of art in the age of mechanical reproduction. Benjamin (1999, 214) notes: "Even in the case of a reproduction that is highly perfected, there is an element lacking: the *hic et nunc* of the work of art—its unique and unrepeatable existence in the place where it is." In fact, "the *hic et nunc* of the original constitutes the concept of its authenticity." This "here and now" of the work of art essentially refers to the ritual context of worship, tied to the temple, which was then substituted by the museum. The magic of the technology abolishes the distance of the *hic et nunc*, triggering in the liturgical act a dynamic for certain verses, similar to those in the mechanical reproduction of the work of art, thanks to which the most faithful reproductions are created in which there is everything except the work itself.

The availability of touch technology, that is, haptic technology, makes this possibility even more tangible. I have already noted that today people interact more and more with devices and machines through touching a screen. The boundaries between users and their electronic devices seem destined to collapse, resulting in a new relationship with an object. The object, that is, the physical device, in this perception disappears in

favor of the experience, which it is able to convey to us. The interaction with the machine is already wireless. The difference between the iPad and the crystal ball is that in the case of the iPad
there is no need for a magic wand, which is, like the mouse and
the keyboard, an abstraction. The finger suffices:[11] everything
on the Web is at one's fingertips (Spadaro 2010a).

Undoubtedly, the rise of touch technology has its consequences: touch technology is tied to the sense most anchored
in the present, the immediate, and the contingent—touch. To
indicate that something is evident, one says that one can "touch
it with one's hand." Fact is becoming what St. Thomas Aquinas, in his *De Anima,* defined as "sensorio commune" (common sense), meaning that faculty of the soul that compares the
different senses, that unifies the sensitive content into a unique
perception, and that refers every sensation to the consciousness
of feeling (Ferraris 2010). In fact, in using an iPad, it is touch
itself that confirms for me what I see on the screen, unifying,
integrating, and synchronizing the other experiences of sense
that I make on the tablet.[12]

Beyond the experience of tablets, like the iPad, we must think
also of the enormous success of video game consoles, like the
Nintendo Wii. Its controler reacts to vector forces and to the
orientation of three-dimensional spaces through a built-in accel-
erometer, causing the avatar on the screen to perform the movements made by the person in front of the screen. Now, Microsoft
has gone further with the three-dimensional video camera, Ki-
nect, a motion-sensing input device that enables users to control and interact with their machine without the need of a
controller, simply by moving in front of the device's "eye."

If we take this peculiar touch and wireless logic inside the
liturgical event, we can better understand the problem, that is,
we ask if the liturgy on the Web is a liturgical event or, instead,
if it is a "technological reproduction" of that same event.

If the example of the difference between a picture and a
print of it is insufficient, then we can also ask ourselves: if I sit
on my couch at home and listen, with a very sophisticated

sound system, to a compact disc recording of a symphony, can I say that I participated in that concert? In reality, the liturgical event is never technologically reproducible, because it incorporates in its *hic et nunc*—in which is celebrated in an unreproducible way the action of the Holy Spirit—which makes the Mystery of Christ present and actualizes it and then, in the Catholic liturgy, the ritual comes from the body. "We do not baptize the neocortical layer of the brain, but the whole body, that quivering mass of nerves, blood, muscles and fibres, of emotions and human sentiments, of hopes and doubts. We belong to a people who exactly belong to a body" (Mitchell 2005, 118; see also O'Leary 2005). The *hic et nunc* of the Web is that of the human who "leaves his [or her] prison, the body, and emerges into a world of digital sensations" (Heim 1991) with an "angelic" nature, that is, as intelligence in action, but without an earthly body (Lévy 1997b, 102)[13]—is this sufficient to realize a liturgical event? Exclusively for the eye, would it not be too textual, individualistic, detached, disembodied? Can what is sufficient for a "techno-pagan" ritual be sufficient for a Catholic liturgy? The negative response is summarized by a declaration of the Secretariat for the Liturgy of the United States' Bishops.[14] They affirm that the celebration of the sacraments requires the "physical" and "geographical" presence, the "presence of all of the people in contact with reality [not simply with an image or an idea] of the saving presence of Christ." Electronic projections "seem to lack the capability to communicate at the level of the word, action and physical perception that are natural for those who are physically present" and they thus generate a "limited presence." To sum up, the liturgical event is not accessible, either digitally or virtually: any of its scansions (in the way that a scanner does, by interpreting an image in the form of pixels) results in something that is not efficacious. In fact, the liturgy always "works" on the body, organizing the spheres of emotions, of sensibility, of actions, in such a way that these spheres will be the presence of the sacred, of the mystery of Christ.

What is the final sense of the objections presented by the American bishops? We believe it is the impenetrable difference between reality and information (Borgmann 1999). A liturgical event's reality is never reducible to the information that we have. This is, in essence, the same logic of incarnation that requires a precarious and transient context, a spatio-temporal situation, a corporal tangibility. The complex *ecology* of the rite is also fundamental to its significance, which, in short, cannot be transferred to the *economy* of the information processes of the media, and of machines in general, as sophisticated as they are in permitting transmission (Borgmann 2003, 126). On the other hand, we must take account of the fact that by the extension of sensibilities, the "machines of relationship" are being transformed into surrogates. Today, many affective relationships, even the most ordinary ones, are mediated by machines. Even in common speech we say "yesterday, I spoke to Stephen" when we mean "yesterday, I called Stephen." Will we extend the expressions "yesterday, I saw Frank" when we mean "yesterday I had a video-chat with Frank on Skype," for instance? Our biological senses seem inadequate to keep pace with the possible conditions of relations that overcome the "here and now." Their expansions by machines tend to assume a normality through which, for example, when the mobile phone has no signal, one has the impression that an important type of relationship is no longer possible and one feels a sense of isolation. If reality cannot be reduced to information, it remains true that information permits some form of participation in the event. We must deepen this participation in the liturgical environment, which is undoubtedly more interactive and engaging than is pure television viewing.

THE LITURGICAL EVENT: BETWEEN
VIRTUAL PRESENCE AND GRAPHIC INTERFACE

The truly problematic nucleus of the question that we are confronting seems to be given by the fact that *virtual* existence appears to be configured with an uncertain ontological status: it leaves aside the physical, but offers a form, that is sometimes also vivid, of social presence. This is unquestionably not simply a product of the conscience, an image of the mind; nor is it a *res extensa*, an ordinary, objective reality, because it also exists only when there is interaction. A world opens before us that is "intermediary" (see Queau 1989), hybrid, and puts the "metaphysics of the presence" under discussion (see Fallon 2009; Levinson 2003). This world needs to be investigated in order to better understand it theologically (see Herring 2008).

The existential spheres included in the presence on the Web are in fact better investigated through their plot. In actuality, the *Second Life* game phenomenon, for example, has three plots (see M. Bittanti 2007, 7). The first life is the dimension of real, concrete life, that is, life that is nondigital and offline. The second life is the life of an avatar in a simulated context, which is why it is called *Second Life*. The third life is an ensemble of the activity of a subject who acts in a simulated context through an avatar. A person in so-called real life who acts in a virtual context is a cyborg (a cybernetic organism), because he/she is empowered through prostheses, both analog and digital, made up of the same avatar, and obviously by the computer, with a monitor and keyboard. This existential plane takes shape in the moment when the subject makes two planes of reality interact, the real one and the digital one.[15] For example, the avatar is a digital extension of the same subject who lives and acts in real life, not an autonomous being or one that is one step away from him- or herself. All of one's freedoms and responsibilities in one's first life are therefore also attributed to one's avatar that lives in the second life. It is the same person who, through his/her avatar, moves within a simulated world. This avatar is not other than oneself. It is always the same person, who is living in a different anthropological space (see Sanavio 2011). Doubtlessly, one part of our capacity to see and listen is clearly already *in* the Web, so the connectivity is already in a phase of definition as a law whose violation will make a profound impression on the relational and social capacity of people. Our same identity is seen ever more clearly as a value to think about in regard to its dissemination in various spaces and not simply as being tied to our physical presence in biological reality.

One line of reflection that appears to be significant in regard to the understanding of the liturgy in the era of digital technology, is that of the philosopher Albert Borgmann, who demonstrated the differences between technical devices—such as radios, television sets, computers, and cell phones—and "focal things," such as the hearth and the shared meal, but also the altar where a liturgy is taking place.[16] Borgmann connects these two contingent cultures with two very different spheres. The first is tied to comfort and control, where the constraints of space, time, traditions, and things do not in themselves have significance beyond their use. In this sense, the air conditioner that warms an environment is a commodity, which we turn off or on as we need it (or which is turned on or off automatically); by contrast, a chimney needs not only a process of preparation, but also provides a broad spectrum that is both symbolic and emotive. A characteristic of focal things, such as the domestic hearth, is that they make the world semantically coherent, requiring an intensive engagement with both the body and the mind, promoting a form of common consciousness like that lived in the context of a celebration, connected in space and time, whose significance cannot ever be resolved in pure information.

From experiments with the liturgy on the Web, therefore, what can we, at least provisionally, assert? That they lack that vision which is aware of the "distance" of the mystery in which we participate, in which we immerse ourselves, thanks to the fact that it gives to us. In its magic way, the look of the Web tends to establish a connection that necessitates an adequate graphic interface without which it is not possible to have true access to the event.[17] The accent falls on the most abstract *operatio* in the greatest measure, and not on the *opus* in its same concreteness. The liturgy and its sacramental dimensions, with their highly symbolic sensibilities, offer a peculiar form of the "graphic interface" of the mystery. In fact, as St. Augustine teaches, it is the invisible *res* and the visible *signa* that are the interface between them in an inseparable tying together. It is therefore an analogical interface and not a digital one. In the digital world, the *res*, "reality," in the measure in which this reality appears on a monitor, "floats" (Borgmann 1999, 5). In fact, I can see the same things on different screens and even copy them at the same time. If we think of the visualization of a Web page simultaneously on several computers, in reality the effect is potentially about what happens when several television sets are turned on at the same time, tuned to a channel that transmits the Sunday mass. In the case of the Web, however, the event is potentially always available; its center is everywhere and borders do not exist. McLuhan's reflection on the microphone returns to us, empowered by the recent technical evolution.

Reality is no longer anchored in the local view or in a superficial, specific visualization. At its center is "an entity virtual, 'de-territorialized,' able to generate many concrete manifestations at different moments and in determined places without being, however, in itself tied to a space or a particular time?" (Lévy 2001, 17)[18]—in short, the form of the real that we call the *virtual*. Theological grace is at the risk of becoming a "commodity," whereas the liturgical celebration is a fact of grace and not of "gratification" (Borgmann 2003, 127). It is because grace stays within logic that it is proper and necessary that the "breaking of bread" should be an event in which we physically participate, in a "focal activity" that "converges our world as would a convex lens, and sends its rays behind it, towards our world, as a concave mirror would" (124).

THE SCREEN'S LOGIC

One may want to consider what is really meant when using the term *screen* in connection with the digital media: the screen is never mere glass (see Lellouche 1997). Glass lets us see what is behind it while separating us from what we see. Fundamentally, it is a good response to the logic of contemplation, which is then presented well in the liturgy, especially in the oriental one, where, in short, the veil covers in order to unveil. With connotations that are less profound and more objectifying, glass separates to join, to make visible what would otherwise not be visible. At times, it takes on a function of containment so we can see: think of an acquarium, for instance. The screen lives with a logic that is completely different. It does not separate to unite, but makes visible what *is not* visible—it makes something that is neither behind it nor within it "appear." The source of information transmitted and visualized on a screen is not *internal* to the screen, *going beyond* itself, and the visual information that it communicates is not tied to it, just as the text is not tied to the page; instead, it "floats" out of it. The screen is not always *substitutable*, but it is *interchangeable*. Whoever looks at the screen does not look *through* it but *into* it, and so what he sees is always an *apparition* and not a *view* or a *vision*. The digital media, especially if connected to the Web, are incised, therefore, on the natural ties between images and reality: "Evidence, as criteria of the truth, seems to lose any significance. Today, the image is an autonomous product that is completely independent of the real, a pure fruit of human creativity" (Vecchi 2010, 19). The view is thus not tied to the concrete: we do not see things but *realities that appear* at a determined moment, and whose visibility is neither stable nor guaranteed.

THE "FLOATING" TEXT AND LITURGICAL RESISTANCE

With the expansion of digital reading with portable tools, like the Amazon Kindle, the text detaches itself in a definitive way from its solid anchorage in the material reality of the page, from its support. Of what, then, does the challenge posed by screens to the comprehension of sacred texts consist? Above all, the written page that appears on the screen is susceptible to wide editorial manipulation. In reality, this manipulation has developed in a way that is becoming freer from the goal of the 1970s, that is, from when photocomposition, which released text from the rigid sequentiality that was tied to the physicality of lead typefaces, began. If the printed word then becomes digital, you can save, edit, or delete it at a click. However, it can, above all, be copied and pasted, and thus duplicated, without any problems. The text is a fluid object that can be modified. It is the exact opposite of the "Laws of the Twelve Tables" and of the said *scripta manent.*

There is, however, a change that is even more radical, which Filippo Tommaso Marinetti and a group of futurist artists had already prefigured in 1916: "the book, the traditional means for conserving and communicating thought, has for a long time been destined to disappear." For them, this is, in fact "the static companion of the sedentary, of the nostalgic." Prophetically, the futurists yearned for "great tables of free words," "luminous mobile signs," a "poly-expressiveness": "We will put in motion the free words that break the limits of literature, marching towards painting, music, the arts of noise." The futurists were talking about cinema, but with their words they were already prefiguring that form of expression which is hypertext language and reading on "tables of words."

More recently Ivan Illich (1993, 3s) concluded that "the alphabetic text is only one of many ways to codify something that is not called the "message."[19] The page is no longer a sort of icon, painted on parchment—as happened at the time of the great, illuminated Bibles—but a screen. The text detaches itself from the material reality of the page. The veneration has been displaced onto the message, onto the text, and the page becomes provisional, the book an accessory. The liturgy, instead, still tends to think of the sacred page as an icon. The page of the Gospel—even if it is no longer richly illuminated as it once was—remains an integral part of the ritual action of the Christian community. It is unimaginable, for example, that one could carry an iPad or a portable computer in a procession. It is unimaginable that a monitor could be solemnly incensed and kissed in a liturgy. Instead, "for the monk, the book is a sacred object that, during the liturgy, is carried around with great solemnity, it is honoured with incense, it is lit by a special candle, and the illumined capital letters are kissed before and after the reading of the step marked by that image" (110). The Catholic liturgy is therefore a bulwark of resistance in the relationship text/page against the volatilization or, perhaps, the "spiritualization" of the text, disembodied from a page of ink.

The page becomes the body of a text that would otherwise remain open and new incarnations and "apparitions" in different forms would always be possible: a click is enough to change formatting, to modify the dimensions of the characters, their color, and their graphic style (the font).

The Church has had to confront other revolutions and evolutions that have touched on the status of the lettered page during its relationship with text throughout the centuries. We might think of the Council of Trent, for example, which embraced the cutting edge technology of its time: the printing press.

All the liturgical books of the Post-Tridentine reform—with the exception of the *Breviarium romanum* of 1568, which ended with the *Rituale romanum* of 1614—were printed works. After all, the technology of the printing press permitted the creation of what became known as *ediciones typicae* or official editions of liturgical rites that could be used as "authorized" models ahead of the other printed texts. This clearly served the Church's intention to create a liturgy that was truly global, that would be (or could be) uniform in all dioceses and parishes (Mitchell 2005, 115).

However, as Illich (1993, 119–31) has shown, the roots date back to the twelfth century, when lettered pages were no longer works of art, or rich, colorful icons locked in sacred books that were illuminated and incensed. The pages, thanks to university professors and mediaeval academics—from Albert the Great to

Bonaventure to Bagnoregio to Thomas Aquinas—became the reason for disputes and argumentation. The text, thanks to the scholastics, was completely independent of the page; the text no longer had the need to be anchored in a physical reality. The text "floated above" the page, ready to be used in the service of scholars' arguments and controversies. The writings thus began to have their own lives, detached from physical objects, and began to live in what we today call "virtual reality" (Mitchell 2005, 116), which Marinetti and the futurists had already foreseen as a "table of words."

We understand how these arguments are able to mold the way of living a liturgical event. An event that occurs on the Web tends to be a spectacle of sorts, an apparition that is always available and replicable. The event can always be covered, in journalistic jargon, by the media: if it is not covered, it is not visible. So, viewing it on the Web can become *phagic*, in the sense that it is free to tend to engulf the event and to take it, to *reduce* it, to its own flow. Fundamentally, if the event *takes shape* on the Web, it is because this seems to subtract it from the world of our primary experience. This can create a type of short circuit between the virtual and the spiritual, in the sense that spiritual is the opposite of physical (see Davis 1999). The landscape—that is, the panorama that is beyond perception and contemplating in which we recognize the landscape—becomes a *simulacra*, that is, an image that has no corresponding reality, of an environment or its own true inscape, namely an interiorized panorama inside of which the mystery is brought back.

AUGMENTED REALITY AND SACRAMENT

Giving us a different vision of that same reality that we have before us, technology permits us to have a type of *optic* view. This already happens with diagnostic tools, such as ultrasound or CAT scans, which allow us to see inside the body, overcoming the physical barriers of the skin. Today, however, so-called augmented reality (AR) is available to everyone. It is made up of the superimposition of levels of information (virtual and multimedia elements, geographically localized data, and so on) in the real experience of our everyday lives.

The elements that augment reality are available on smartphones, like the iPhone or Android phones. Concretely, one can use an AR application—like Layar, NearestWiki, Robotvision, Accrosair, Blippar, or others—and can thus orient the objective in any direction: on a smartphone screen we can see an image of a location, including information about the place that we are seeing, its history, and also the presence of shops, cafés, and other markers.

In this case, the view does not contemplate reality, capturing the maximum of the information that it contains, but it superimposes virtual reality on actual reality; this virtual reality is made up of flows of information that stand outside the same reality that I see, so I can better understand it. There exist, for example, applications that use the geographical coordinates of places and remarkable objects (for example, works of art), described in Wikipedia, so as to integrate them into AR applications. Now, the faith that discerns the body of Christ in a host raised by the priest in the Eucharistic celebration furnishes information that is additional to what my eyes already see, generating a perception that is made up of a "mixed reality," as it has been defined.

The question is: Can, by analogy, the light that the faith offers to the everyday lives of believers be understood as a form of augmented reality? Do people's uses of AR influence the perception and practice of the sacraments? The first impact may be generated by individuals in the use of the device, which is opposed to the social life of the Church, within which the sacrament is celebrated. The sacraments are always *of the* Church, because Christ works in this, and *for* the Church, that is, they make the Church itself. The Church acts as a community in the sacraments. These are visible signs and in them the grace of Christ acts. The faith is not just information that can discern

Christ's body in the bread but is expressed, nourished, and strengthened by the sacraments.

On one level, we find that we are impeded by looking at faith in the same way as at an information device. On another, the sacrament is a visible and effective sign of grace; it does not, therefore, just generate information, but it *makes* what it *says*. This is its nature as an *effective sign* theologically (and not psychologically in as much as it is active *ex opera operato*) which radically distinguishes it from any possible form of augmented reality, which is mediated by a screen and visualizes information that comes from the outside.

For some, augmented reality is already becoming a new metaphor for telling the way in which contemporary humans can understand faith in as much as he/she can understand faith as a means to learn and live his/her ordinary experience (my life, the life of the world). Hearing the Word of God through the Bible has just this function; it is enough to read Psalm 119.105—"Thy word is a lamp unto my feet, and a light unto my path, O Deuteronomy" and who asks to place the Lord's precepts as "frontlets between [thine] eyes" (Deuteronomy 6.8)—to see reality in an "augmented" way, to be precise, by the faith. Reflection on this and on the development of this metaphor has just begun.[20]

PROBLEMS AND CHALLENGES OF PRYING ONLINE

The key question is whether digital technologies are redefining the sense of the presence and of the presence beyond contemporaneity. After having affirmed the reality of the sacrament, the question about how the habit for virtuality can in some way have an effect on that same comprehension of the sacrament, as well as on the way it is lived, is still open (Casey 2006).

A perhaps useful comparison for this comprehension is that between theater and cinema. In the theater, the interpreter presents him- or herself to the public in the first person. In the cinema, "the artistic performance of the cinematographic actor is instead presented through equipment" (Benjamin 1999, 222).

So, the actor in the *hic et nunc* acts for a machine and not for a public. Then the public uses it, thanks to technical equipment. The priest who celebrates a liturgy in virtual reality thus does not celebrate it for a public but for a piece of technical apparatus that makes his action present to the public who participates in the liturgy. At this point, there are two important elements that complete my considerations: First, the logic that causes the actor to become a *divo,* or the politician who becomes a dictator when put on the spot, can also cause the priest to become a wizard through his experience of the divine (Giaccardi 2010). Second, the protagonist in a Web event is always, in a peculiar and accentuated way, a product that has to be presented to others in an aesthetically pleasing way, letting them know about a type of autopresentation that is always a performance.

Undoubtedly, the Web experience cannot be reduced to its extremes and to the dangers that it exposes. Furthermore, this is increasingly understood as a peculiar form of experience and not as a surrogate. Is this all a blunder? Probably not. In fact, digital and telematic technologies have created a new space of experience, just as all the major technologies of the past, which Christian worship has had to adapt to.

Pierre Lévy (2001, 194) urges us to take the example of photography so as to better comprehend what is happening. Photography, in fact, has not become a substitute for painting, even if it has made the "optical capture" of a scene easier and faster. Where once paintbrushes, pigments, and an ability to draw were necessary to capture an image, now all that is needed is a small camera and no particular skill. Photography allows us to do the same thing as before—namely, to represent something—but faster and with greater simplicity. It allows us, above all, to perceive in a new and different way that takes us to the development of new functions. Photography has permitted also the deployment of new functions of the image, which has had repercussions for painting. Will this not also be so for the experience of the Web in general, and therefore also for experience that is tied to religious worship? Here, this opens a possible path to the deepening of a new area of experience that is still in the process of being defined and comprehended, of a new plane of existence that requires its own peculiar form of religious expression, even of communal prayer. More specifically: humans on the Web express their desire to pray, and even to have a liturgical life. Reflections are actually born and the questions that we are facing emerge from empirical evidence and from the evaluation of experiences.

At this point, the correct attitude would be not only that of *defending* the richness of the liturgy itself, so that we can still understand it, but in understanding how the desire for God, overpowering in this new plane of existence and also in search of forms of expression, emerged. Today, in the era of the Web, the challenges to the comprehension of the sacraments and liturgical celebrations by believers remain evident, considering that "the liturgy can be deemed the code of codes, the assumption of every other mediatic code and paradigm of every authentic communication."[21]

In particular, if sacramental logic implies *matter*, understood as a susceptible element, in cyberspace is it possible to develop a dynamic equivalent to matter? The Web requires electricity, which is a form of energy (see Herring 2005, 45): In what way and in what form can it be lived inside of what is still a wide dynamic of sacramental values? The rite will always remain constantly tied to the basics and the basic necessities of life (water, food, oil, washing oneself, feeding oneself, anointing oneself, and so on). These elements and behaviors are carried out in the rite so as to be elements in life and language, to give them sense. Electricity is already an integral part of our ordinary lives. Witness, for example, the prayer of benediction for a power plant that we read in the Blessings of the Roman Rite:

> Lord God, all powerful, creator of light, source and origin of every being, look upon your children who have realized this new work for the production of energy in service of the human community;

allow us always to seek your face, beyond the shadows of this world, can come to you, indefectible light, in which we live, move and have our being, today and always. (No. 983)

Above all, the question remains (Robinson-Neal 2008): How does the virtual experience change the person who is the subject of the "actual" liturgy, that of our celebrations in the church, stimulating some potentialities and inhibiting others? Marshall McLuhan, at the beginning of the 1970s, speaking of the culture of the media, had already understood well that "the changes imposed by the cultural transformation that we are going through also profoundly touch the liturgy" (McLuhan 1999, 149).[22]

CHAPTER 6

The Technological Tasks
of Collective Intelligence

Today, more than ever before, the spread of digital technologies permits people to remain connected, that is, to have the possibility of opening with ease, immediacy, and at accessible costs (if not for free) channels of communication that are able to break down geographical and economic barriers and bridge distances. It used to be that we would open and then close a connection when, for example, sending a letter, making a telephone call, or sending a fax; the expansion of the web of digital transmissions, however, makes it possible for people to be virtually always discoverable, that is open to receiving communication from others. The ensemble of the Web signifies that it makes up an invisible space of knowledge, of the potentiality of thought. It will constitute—together with a technological system for communicating and thinking—a sort of intelligence that is distributed everywhere and that is growing continually. The Internet, in fact, provides the infrastructure to connect resources, time, content, and ideas. The classic example is Wikipedia, which, beyond any valuation, is the fruit of the convergence of many connected people, who think and write. The Web's wiring gives life to an emerging and vital force, able to collect delocalized and fragmented knowledge and aggregate it. The intellectually collaborative organization emerges from the Web as a phenomenon that, albeit not radically new, is undoubtedly of ample proportions. Today, one thinks and one knows the world not only in the traditional manner, through reading and exchange or within the confines of special interest groups (for example, teaching or study groups), but through realizing a vast connection between people. Intelligence is distributed everywhere and it can be easily interconnected. The Web gives life to a form of *collective intelligence.* The Church itself recognizes that it has a responsible role in the "formation of a human collective culture" (Müller 2010).

HOW DOES PIERRE LÉVY THINK
COLLECTIVE INTELLIGENCE?

This interconnected intelligence has made someone imagine the perspective of a unique body that, feeding on connections, is explained as a thinking unity. The greatest theoretician of this vision of collective intelligence is the philosopher Pierre Lévy (1997b), professor in the Department of Hypermedia at the University of Paris VIII, Saint-Denis. This vision, which seems so innovative and tied to our times, would have been unthinkable in the past. In reading Lévy, we must take into account that the foundations of his thought are rooted in the past. The collective intelligence realized by the Web, in fact has theological roots that date back to mediaeval times. Lévy bases his theory on the comprehension of intelligence on the Web on the neoplatonic theology of the Islamic philosophers of the eleventh century, including Al-Fârâbi and Ibn Sina, better known as Avicenna. If it is difficult to summarize the complexity and rich philosophy of these authors, it is undoubtedly possible to single out a central focus in their philosophy. At the heart of their anthropology is the idea of a unique and separate intelligence, identified through all of the human species, that could be considered a communal intellect, a collective consciousness. It seems, therefore, that the first to take up the sense and value of collective intelligence were the Arab philosophers I have already mentioned. Their thought is therefore in a phase of rediscovery, helped through the birth of modern science and philosophy, and the resultant gnoseological question is totally different. It seems that their philosophies will make recent innovations more "thinkable."

The common reasoning in such a picture is conceived as a conjunction between God and human beings; it is self-thinking thought, thought that thinks itself: pure creative intelligence. The intelligence of humans is tied to God through a unique and separate intelligence, because it is an intelligence that is always in action. This intellect is a sort of collective consciousness; this consciousness uninterruptedly contemplates true ideas that are put into action, that is, it makes them effective. Human intelligence emanates toward them all of the ideas that they can perceive and contemplate. Here, it is not a case of further deepening the complex dynamic of this theological vision; in reality, the collective intellect is only the tenth intelligence inside a descending process of the emanation from God of separate intelligences that follow one another, each one turns to and desires that of the one that precedes it. This tension upward puts the heavens in an eternal motion, because the lower intelligences never reach the higher intelligences they desire. All of the celestial hierarchies are therefore implicated in the smallest act of knowledge.[1]

WHAT IS THEOLOGICAL, BECOMES TECHNOLOGICAL

Lévy was inspired by this vision, which is undoubtedly very suggestive, even in its complexity, and this spotlight, that operates on a conversion from the transcendent to the immanent, from theology to anthropology. In inverting the terms of the schema, God is transmuted into an open possibility for human development; the angelic or celestial world becomes the region of the virtual worlds, through which human beings are in *intellectual collectivity*; the intellect becomes the space for the communication and navigation of individual members of the collective intelligence.

More precisely, if the "celestial hierarchies" of the Islamic schema open up space for the communication of humanity with itself, in parallel, the "virtual worlds" put intelligences and accompanying individuals and groups in the collective consciousness into communication. From the concrete intelligences and sharing of a multitude of little groups, a virtual world emerges that offers them greater variety and gives them new possibilities for these groups. This world expresses a collective intelligence. In its turn, it is the virtual world that illuminates the individuals.[2] In agreeing with Avicenna, Lévy encourages direct contact with collective thought. If theology drew up a schema with unidirectional diffusion, descending and then centrifugal, Lévy's anthropological inversion foresees a centripetal circulation, which then ascends: "What was theological, becomes technological" (Lévy 1997b, 52).

To explain the significance of the Web, Lévy seeks to use a complex theological discourse, putting in its place a technological device, overturning everything and substituting what was on high, God, with what was at the bottom, that is, the human community that generates virtual worlds. Lévy writes:

> Instead of emitting to men the intellectual light that comes from God via the heavens and the higher angels, the virtual world performs the role of the intellect, reflecting the flashes that come from the human community, the intelligences of a multitude of individuals and little groups, angelic regions of a new type. Virtual worlds that thus emanate from intellectual collectivities and take their existence only from the human community from which they proceed, all that in theological discourse proceeded from top to bottom must be translated into the socio-technical device, like a jet from the bottom to the top. (99–100)

In this system, transcendence becomes a temptation. However, Lévy's insistence in negating the transcendence confirms that the system made reference to a theological dimension; in this case it was a hypostatization of the gnostic character of the same human community. Lévy here intuits something that seems to be decisive: the reflections on the intelligence being developed on the Web itself, and these reflections must have a theological dimension. To think of the intelligence developed by these single intelligences that are connected on the Web signifies thinking "in the form of theology." It is in this thought that one can read an eschatological proclamation, although it is proclaimed in the guise of a new form of social utopia with a Marxist imprint. This, in fact, is the logical consequence: the individual becomes a hardware terminal of sorts compared to a collective intelligence that thinks anywhere and at any time about creation of their common world.

PIERRE TEILHARD DE CHARDIN AND THE PATH TO THE NOOSPHERE

Lévy's reasoning challenges us to ask, how does one think the common intelligence among humans? His solution is to adopt the theological neoplatonic, Islamic schema, because this seemed to him to be suitable for furnishing categories of thought. His strategy was to overturn the theological nature to make it become anthropological and sociological, leading to outcomes that are Marxist in character. One of the major problems of this schema is the role of individuals inside the system. The challenge is, therefore, the following: Will it be possible to think of a form of communal intelligence without it becoming *"collective"* assuming the traits of a collectivist and depersonalized utopia?

Derrik De Kerckhove—professor at the University of Toronto (Canada) and at the University of Napoli-Federico II (Italy), where he teaches the sociology of digital culture—has sought to integrate the approach of his friend Lévy, preferring the definition of "connective intelligence" over "collective intelligence," enhancing the practices, the opening of the connections, rather than the collectivist dimension. However, the challenge remains open.[3] Prior to Lévy, the religious genius who—although he did not resolve some of the shadows and ambiguities—best took up this challenge was the Jesuit priest Pierre Teilhard de Chardin.[4] He did this—by intuitions that are, in their way, prophetic, given that he died in 1955—through his concept of the *noosphere*, which is developed through the interaction of human beings, hand in hand, who populated the Earth and then (and who still are) organizing themselves into forms of complex social networks.

In his reflections, Teilhard de Chardin (2008) talks about the history of the world from a very dynamic perspective of evolution, with a design that comes from a distance, from the creation, and looks far ahead, toward the Omega Point of history, where the resurrection of Christ summarizes the meaning of all of history. It passes through different states: we have beneath our feet a lithosphere, a first stage in the evolution of our planet, a nucleus that is still without life. However, around this is developing a film that is thin but externally dynamic, which is the biosphere, the birthplace of life, both animal and vegetable, which man then follows.

A new stratum, little by little, is also forming on our planet. It is at first fragile and thin, like a small cobweb, then becoming ever more intense, a dense mesh of relationships, of communications of thought and knowledge. Teilhard de Chardin's vision includes the story of man that signals a progressive aggregation: from the first, in the form of groups of scattered hunters here and there, then as groups of farmers and, then, of the first civilizations and the first empires. Now all is in contact and is moved by "a wave of 'participation' that shakes the social and ethnic masses profoundly" to an always greater convergence, a consciousness that includes all of humanity and that is also helped in its development by machines (Teilhard de Chardin 1969, 173–74). Here, Teilhard de Chardin speaks of the noosphere, the sphere of knowledge and thought. In the past it was only embryonic, very fragile, but then it became much thicker and frequently very dense. We are immersed in this sphere in which messages produced by thought and human intelligence are passed in all directions. He writes:

> In the first place, I think, naturally, of the extraordinary Web of radiophonic and televisual communications that, perhaps anticipating a direct syntonysation of brains, mediate by the still mysterious forces of telepathy. Now, we already correlate all of it into a type of "etherised consciousness." However, I also think of the insidious ascent of those surprising calculating machines that, thanks to signals combined in reasoning at some hundreds of thousands per second, will not only free our brains from hard, exhausting work, but will also augment in us the essential factors (which are often little observed) of the "rapidity of thought," we are preparing a revolution in the research field. (174)

In order to understand the flow of the prophetic vision of this discourse, we must remember that this text was first published in 1947. Here, Teilhard de Chardin attributed to technological communications a fundamental role in the creation of a communal consciousness, of a sort of brain constituted by interconnections, not of nonthinking fibres, but of other thinking brains (256). In this sphere, Teilhard de Chardin is extremely ambiguous about what actually does move, yet, we are definitely immersed within it. Teilhard de Chardin sees the world as a large and interconnected Web that points toward salvation.

Teilhard de Chardin's language is much more helpful than any synthesis. In *The Spiritual Phenomenon,* published in 1937, he writes:

> Atoms ourselves, we at first see only other atoms. But it does not require much reflexion to discover that animate bodies are not as separate from one another as they appear. Not only are they all, by the mechanism of reproduction, related by birth. But by the very process of their development, a network of living connexions (psychological, economic, social, etc.) never for a moment ceases to hold them in a single tissue, which becomes more complicated and tenacious the further they evolve. Like drops of water scattered in the sand and subjected to the same pressure, that of the layer to which they belong; like electrical charges distributed along a single

conductor and subjected to the same potential; so conscious beings are in truth only different local manifestations of a mass which contains them all. To the extent that it is subject to experiment, the phenomenon of spirit is not a divided mass; it displays a general manner of being, a collective state peculiar to our world. In other words, scientifically speaking, there are no spirits in nature. But there is a spirit, physically defined by a certain tension of consciousness on the surface of the earth. This animated covering of our planet may with advantage be called the biosphere—or more precisely (if we are only considering its thinking fringe) the noosphere. (95)

A PLANETARY NERVOUS SYSTEM

Teilhard de Chardin had theorized the notion of the technological, planetary nervous stystem. He had further understood that technologies also enable a sort of interconnected intelligence. He also echoed the images that had already emerged as a result of the expansion of an electricity infrastructure in the second half of the nineteenth century. In 1851, the writer Nathaniel Hawthorne asked whether

> by means of electricity, the material world had not become a great bunch of nerves that vibrate by hundreds and hundreds of thousands in no time? Or, better, all the globe is an immense head, a brain, instinct and intelligence together! Or, rather, we can say that it is this same thought, nothing other than thought, and not the material that we believe! (Hawthorne 2009)

These words were written around the time when Ernst Werner von Siemens invented a model of a telegraph with wires, founding Siemens, which since then has grown into a multinational engineering and electronics conglomerate. It should come as no surprise that these words were written by a literary man, because it is literature itself, from the pages of Hugo to those of Verne, which in those years produced the most vivid descriptions of the electric revolution. These narrations that ideally

linked electric wires and bunches of nerves will be taken from
the literary critic and mass media scholar Marshall McLuhan
when he affirmed that "electric technology is in direct relationship with our nervous systems" (McLuhan 1964/2004, 47, 491).
Today, we can say that in some measure this collective intelligence has been enabled by telematics, the communication connections of the Web, and produces an implosion of the too
rigid distinction between natural and artificial evolution. Teilhard de Chardin spoke of a reality "in which all of the individual thoughts are immersed and are reciprocally influenced
to form with their related multiplicity, a unique Spirit of the
Earth" (Teilhard de Chardin 1970, 40). He saw the world enclosed in its spherical dimensions and inhabited by human beings who increasingly connect with and come closer to each
other, until a compression is developed that raises humanity
and which develops a force of expansion. With the inventions
of yesterday—the railway, the automobile, the airplane—the
physical influence of every man, reduced once to a few miles, is
now extended to thousands of miles. Better yet: thanks to the
discovery of electromagnetic waves, every individual now finds
him- or herself (actively and passively) present at the same time
in all of the seas and continents, coextensive with the Earth.
Humanity grows but in a circumscribed, spherical place, find-
ing itself irremediably subject to a formidable pressure that grows
uninterruptedly through its own play: because every new degree
of compression has the unique effect of magnifying even more
the expansion of every individual element.

In his own time, Teilhard de Chardin (2008, 264) already
had asked: "What would humanity become if, to be absurd, it
had perhaps been free to thin out and expand indefinitely on
an unconfined surface, in other terms, if it had perhaps been
abandoned only to the one game of interior affinities?" Today,
the Web really seems to express a tension toward an indefinite
expansion, a "distinct centre radiating from the heart of a system
of centres." Teilhard de Chardin's vision, however, should not
be confounded with that confounded with Lévy. Teilhard de

Chardin (1970, 115) requires "a quality and a special education of the sight," to which he reaches through a "prolonged meditation" to gather a "cosmically profound sense to certain correlations that use has habituated us to consider superficial." The risks of misunderstanding are high. For Teilhard de Chardin this convergence can be understood as an annulment of the personal dimensions. The second is that God himself can be understood as the "fruit" of this final convergence, according to Lévy's schema.

Teilhard de Chardin is very clear on this, and it is here that we find his strength and originality. The convergent tensions, about which he writes, do not foresee the annulment of the personal dimensions into a sort of homogenization of the consciousness. The supreme consciousness, "just to be supreme, must not cause itself, to the maximum degree, what is the perfection of ours: the illuminating folding of the being into itself?" (2008, 241). In various places in his work, Teilhard de Chardin reiterates that "each elementary person contains in his essence, something unique and untransmittable" (1970, 261), thus addressing the weak point in Marxist theory, on which Lévy's theory is based or, at least, its own outlook (see Coffy 1968). In the Marxist vision, the individual risks becoming a "worker," a "nervous cell" in a system of machines that are outside his or her control and comprehension, an appendix of sorts to a technological process that is governed by capital. The tensions are the "simple" emancipation of these forces from the constraints of private ownership in view of the realization of a "paradise" on earth, founded on successive conquests that each of us, dying, will abandon. Lévy has adapted this vision of virtual capitalism, which Marx could not foresee, and to do this he used mediaeval Islamic theology to overturn Marx's vision of capitalism. Instead, Teilhard de Chardin (2008, 243) invites us to reflect: "This means that the inventions, the education and every type of expression, emanate from each of us and that they will be transferred to the human mass is vitally important." Teilhard de Chardin continues by asking:

What precisely is, in the interests of life in general, the work of human works, if not the constitution, operated by each of us in itself, of an absolutely original centre, in which the Universe is reflected in a unique way, inimitable: our "I," our personality? Here, the focus itself of our conscience, deeper in all its rays: is the essence that Omega must recover in order to be truly Omega. Now, we evidently cannot divest ourselves of this essential part in favour of the others, so that we give a coat, or pass a torch: because we, we are the flame, my "I," to be able to communicate, must be able to subsist in this abandonment, which it makes itself, otherwise the gift vanishes.

This great connective vision thus finally sees each conscience remaining aware of itself. "It is not only conservation, but the exaltation of the elements through convergence . . . in what ever field—which means of cells in a body, or of members of a society, or of the elements of a spiritual synthesis" (244). And again, with an image: "In the flow according to the line of centres, the granules of conscience do not tend to lose their contours and to mix them. They accentuate, instead, the profundity and the incommunicability of their ego. The more, they become, altogether, the Other, the more they individually become 'self'" (ibid.). Jennifer Cobb, who has explicitly created a bridge between the Teilhardian theological vision and the digital environment, seeing in cyberspace a clear expression of the noosphere, affirms: "The levels of information and of global connectivity that are available through cyberspace can strengthen our experiences of 'harmonized complexity,' the experiences of being at the same time free to express the uniqueness of our 'I' while we participate in a context that is synthetic and global" (Cobb 1998, 96).

A EUCHARISTIC WEB

The Teilhardian vision proposes a clear direction toward which this Web of relationships lifts the world: the noosphere is expanding itself to a growing integration and unification that will culminate in what Teilhard de Chardin defines as the

Omega Point, which is the end of history. The Omega Point is the height of complexity and of conscience, and is independent of the universe that is evolving, and it is thus "transcendent." It is the Logos, namely Christ, through whom all things were made. The convergence in Christ is the force that guides human and cosmic evolution and which models the universe toward a level of conscience that is in constant expansion.[5]

The Omega Point is not an abstract idea, but a personal being, that unites creation, magnetically attracting it toward itself: it is "a distinct Centre radiating from the heart of a system of centres" (Teilhard de Chardin 2008, 244). This Omega Point does not constitute the result of the complexities and of the consciences. It is, therefore, in no way the *sum* of human beings, preexisting in the evolution of the universe, because it is the cause of the evolution of the universe toward the major complexities, consciences, and personalities, and the point of convergence is the center of transcendent attractions.

> God exerts pressure, in us and upon us—through the intermediary of all the powers of heaven, earth and hell—only in the act of forming and consummating Christ, who saves and sur-animates the world. *And since, in the course of this operation, Christ himself does not act as a dead or passive point of convergence, but as a centre of radiation* for the energies which lead the universe back to God through his humanity, the layers of divine action finally come to us impregnated with his organic energies. (Teilhard de Chardin 1967, 123)

In his vision of humanity and the universe as an enormous connective Web, Teilhard de Chardin sees in Christ one who gives movement and direction to unity, and this vision clearly has a Eucharistic dynamic (see Tilliette 2008, 127–35): "When the priest says: '*Hoc est Corpus meum*', the words fall directly onto the bread and directly transform it into the individual reality of Christ. But the great sacramental operation does not cease at that local and momentary event" (Teilhard de Chardin 1967, 123–24), it extends through "the vast multitudes of men in every epoch and in every land" (124). The Eucharistic Christ controls the entire movement of the universe, the Christ *"per quem Omnia, Domine, semper creas, vivificas et praestas nobis"* in this way, "the Eucharistic transformation goes beyond and completes the Transubstantiation of the bread on the altar. Gradually and irresistibly sweeping the Universe" (125). The point where this process and the noosphere mature in Teilhard de Chardin's vision coincides with Parousia.

A CONVERGENT INTELLIGENCE

Through his reflections, Pierre Lévy helps to verify how thinking about today's technological innovation would be arduous without a theological mindset. It is not a question of principle, but of fact. To think about the Web and the impact of new technologies on humans, we need categories that only theological thought seems able to furnish. However, distorting theology overturns it, as Lévy has done. It signifies the generation of a utopia of totalitarian traits. Instead, Teilhard de Chardin's rich and complex vision seems, even with all its ambiguities, to be rich with prophetic impulses. This proposes an open vision of transcendence that is able to understand an intelligence that is not "collective" but "convergent" (Teilhard de Chardin 1969, 291). With his creative and poetic language, Teilhard de Chardin was uniquely able to express these ideas that were otherwise inexpressible in his time: "Humanity, as I have said, is building its composite beneath out eyes. May it not be that tomorrow, through the logical and biological deepening of the movement drawing it together, it will find its *heart*, without which the ultimate wholeness of its powers of unification can never be fully achieved?" (124). Teilhardian thought, unbalanced eschatologically, displaces the same accents of theological reflection onto the Web's own logic. Theological intuition manifests and sees a magnetic attraction that starts at the end and from outside history, and which gives reason to and values all of the efforts of human minds in social networks; networks that are ever more complex and that not only do not exclude individuality but, on the contrary, enhance it. The Internet becomes a stage in humanity's journey, humanity that is moved, urged on, and guided by God. In this sense, Teilhard de Chardin gives the significance of faith to the Internet's own dynamics within its anthropological space, which at this point can also be understood as part of a unique divine milieu, of that unique "divine environment" which is our world.

Notes

I. THE INTERNET: BETWEEN THEOLOGY
AND TECHNOLOGY

1. See, for example, http://www.historyofyork.org.uk/themes/therailway-revolution.

2. Which is the definition of the existential context in the pastoral orientation of the Italian episcopate for the decade 2010–20 (Pompili 2011, 119).

3. However, the so-called Internet of things is already on the horizon, and thanks to this it will be possible to monitor an environment with a web of small sensors inserted into objects.

4. Push technology allows us to receive updated data every time data changes without any need to explicitly request an update. The classic example is the push notification that one has new e-mail.

5. In this regard we must turn to the broad reflections of the American sociologist and urbanizer Lewis Mumford who, in his *Technics and Civilization* (1963, first published 1934) wrote a story about the machine and its effects on humankind and the consequent relationships between knowing and knowing how to make.

6. To understand the development of the Church's thoughts on communication, one has to read the various documents and reflections

produced on the subject over the course of time. One of the fundamental works in this regard is the collection of 842 Church documents from the Acts of the Apostles to 1973 (the year of its publication)
that were brought together by the Jesuit Father Enrico Baragli (n.d.,
195–210). See also Eilers and Giannatelli (1996), a collection of texts
from 1936–96, and Cebollada (2005), which contains documents
from 1766 to 2005.

7. Ken Bedell (1999) has singled out six types of ecclesial presence
on the Web, based on the balance between the two elements: information and communication.

8. One should also remember Walter Ong's (1967) reflections on
the relationship between systems of communication and cognitive
processes. His reflections are mainly concentrated on orality and theology. See also Ong (1969). For the impact of the teaching of theology, see Soukup, Buckley, and Robinson (2001, 366–77) and Foley
(2005, 45–56).

9. For the complete text (in Italian) go to http://www.vatican.va/
holy_father/paul_vi/speeches/1964/documents/hf_p-vi_spe_1964
0619_analisi-linguistica_it.html.

10. In 1985, noting the growing interaction between technology
and electronics that was moving in the direction of a "New World
Order" of communication, the Pope had already warned that this
change "involves the whole cultural universe, social and spiritual of
the human person" (John Paul II, 1985).

11. The term *cyberspace* was coined by William Gibson in his
1984 science-fiction novel *Neuromancer*. The definition cited is from
Pierre Lévy (2001). He understands the ensemble of electronic communication systems in the way they gather information from digital sources, or through digitalization. Lévy insists on digital coding
because "it conditions the plastic, fluid, calculable, real-time, hy-
pertextual, interactive and, yes, virtual nature of information,
which is, in my opinion, the distinctive characteristic of cyberspace" (74).

12. Lévy (2001, 92) writes, drily, that what is theological becomes
technological in its collective intelligence. Yet, the "theological"
functions of technoscience appear to be, in reality, many and obvious, as shown, for example, in Formenti (2008, 14). A proof of this
is, perhaps, what seems to have been a sort of canonization of Steve
Jobs, in whose death we became involved. For the first time we were

witness to a mass "canonization" of the CEO of a hardware and software company that has attracted a strong, loyal following.

13. For a development of these ideas, see Soukup (2002, 131–43).

14. For a synthesis of the field of study combining communication and theology, see also Soukup (2006, 121–46) and Felton (1989, 17–23).

15. See http://www.radiovaticana.org/it1/Articolo.asp?c=436054.

16. I use the term *impact* with caution and share Lévy's (2001, 3) thoughts: "Technology is compared to a projectile (stone, shell or missile) and the culture or society to a living target. This ballistic metaphor can be criticized on more than one account. It is not so much a question of evaluating the stylistic relevance of a rhetorical figure as it is of updating the way we read phenomena—inadequate as far as I am concerned—revealed by the impact metaphor."

17. See, for example, the chapter "Verso un'intelligenza digitale" (Towards a Digital Intelligence) in Ferri (2011, 72–91). Many works have been written that have discussed the theme of intelligence in the age of the Web. See, for example, Gardner (1983, 2006), Brockman (2011), Carr (2011), Schirrmacher (2010), or Watson (2011).

18. On this subject, see Musso (2007) and De Biase (2003).

19. See the debate on the theme of forgiveness in the age of the Web, in relation to oblivion, which already has a discrete bibliography. See also Mayer-Schönberger (2011).

20. See Højsgaard (2005, 50–63) and Spadaro (2001, 15–27).

21. According to Davis (1995), technopaganism is a type of paganism that uses technological devices in its magic rituals.

22. See http://www.cybertheology.net.

23. Here, reflections on contextual theology appear to be very interesting and illuminating, even though, in the end, they are insufficient, because they always consider the Web as a separate space. See, for example, Herring (2005, 149–65). For the Web as a new existential context, see Pompili (2010).

24. Within the scope of this book, it is impossible to discuss the principles of reflection on the pastoral aspects of the Web. Only two journals have offered interesting contributions in monograph form: *Internet and Church*, an issue of *Credere Oggi*, XXX (2011), 3, and *Monde virtuel, nouveaux médias,* an issue of *Lumen Vitae*, LXVI (2011), 3.

25. "Media Parables" was the title of a National Conference organized by the Italian Bishops' Conference, November 7–9, 2002. This talk was given at the final session.

2. THE HUMAN BEING: DECODER
AND SEARCH ENGINE FOR GOD

1. It is still useful to consult Bull (2000) on this. See also Dini (2005).

2. See Benedict XVI's (2012) Message for the XLVI World Day of Social Communication, which focused on the theme of listening. For the pope, silence and the world are "two moments of communication that must be balanced, followed and integrated." In particular, he reminds us that today too much attention is paid to those who talk, and we forget that true communication is about listening and dialogue, which are both made up of rhythms of words and silence. He thus notes that, on the Web human beings express their need for silence: "We should consider with interest the various forms of sites, applications and social networks, that can help today's man to live moments of reflection and authentic questioning, but also to find spaces of silence, occasions for prayer, meditation and sharing the Word of God."

3. The fact that we can always carry all of our music on one device gives rise to the phenomenon of mobile privatization, through which the environment that is created by the music is the domestic one, which helps us, wherever we are, to not be exposed to the outside, the external, but to perceive ourselves to be at home. See Bonini (2010, 72–84).

4. On the impact of search engines on our social and cultural lives, see, for example, Halavais (2009) and Bottazzini (2010).

5. See http://www.beliefnet.com.

6. These notions were expressed by then Cardinal Ratzinger in his talk at the "Parabole Mediatiche" conference.

7. See http://www.google.com/insidesearch/features/instant/about .html.

8. Another risk that is relevant and that should be noted is that both social networks (like Facebook) and search engines (like Google) retain information about their users, and this data is used to predict results and update personal interests. It is as though Google constructs our profile of interests based on our past use of the Web: the sites we have visited in the past and what interests us most. All of this is anonymously analyzed through reference algorithms, so our searches are never neutral, or based on exclusively objective criteria; instead their results are based on our specific interests. They are sub-

ject specific, and thus different individuals obtain different results even if they use the same search terms. The advantage is immediate: what is presumed to interest me most arrives first, because Google "knows" me and suggests the things that might interest me most. On the other hand, there is a great risk: that of remaining enclosed in a bubble of sorts, from which I would be unable to access that which does not correspond to my profile and my interests, that is, to things that express an opinion different from my own. In the end, I will therefore be surrounded by a world of information that resembles me at the risk of remaining closed to the intellectual provocation that arises from alterity and difference. See Pariser (2011).

9. See http://techcrunch.com/2010/09/12/search-for-god.

10. See http://www.thechurchofgoogle.org.

11. See http://www.wolframalpha.com. For a comparison of the differences between Google and Wolfram|Alpha, see http://www .differencebetween.net/technology/difference-between-google-and -wolfram-alpha/.

3. THE MYSTICAL AND CONNECTIVE BODY

1. For more information on the nature and characteristics of social networks, see Spadaro (2010b).

2. This risk has been emphasized by Sherry Turkle (2011); it is that of creating a relationship on the Web that ends in us passing many hours in digital friendships, while staying at home alone. See also J. Lynch (2011). The category of "taking care of oneself" in a digital context is applied to the sort of relationships that we find in Grotti (2010).

3. For example, Orkut, Qzone, Maktoob, Cloob, Zing, Hyves, Draugiem, Odnoklassniki, Mixi, V Kontakte.

4. The transformation of sociality takes place on the Web. See Castells (2010, 116).

5. The term *Generation Y* was used for the first time in August 1993, in an editorial in the magazine *Ad Age* to describe and distinguish contemporary teenagers from their teen predecessors, "Generation X." Generation Y teens also have been referred to as "millennials." See also Howe and Strauss (2000) and Livingstone and Haddon (2009). A reflection on the faith of this generation can be found in Collins-Mayo et al. (2010).

6. See Estes (2009), Rice (2009), and Cook and Thomas (2011).

7. McLuhan's book was originally published in 1973. It would be interesting to reflect on the origin of Vatican Radio and Pius XI's attitude at the moment he signed the Lateran Pacts on February 11, 1929. This Pope had little interest in real, actual territory. Vatican City is about 110 acres. The motive for having Vatican City was simple, and he made it explicit on that same day in a talk to the parish priests of Rome. He said that sovereign territory was necessary, since "in the world, at least to today, we know of no other forms of sovereignty that are truly our own, if they are not actually territorial." If there had perhaps been another form of territory, he might have chosen that. That is why, though, the Pope really wanted to have the railway and the radio, understanding that the Church's territory is the world and that only the powerful and global media, at that time mainly the radio, could give the sovereignty he desired to the Church. For this, he called Marconi, radio's inventor. The state could be very small, but that would be enough, since with this land it was possible to have both a railway station and an independent radio station. Above all, we must pay attention to the words with which Piux XI blessed the tools of Vatican Radio: "*benedic hanc machinarum seriem ad etheris undas ciendas ut apostolica verba cum longinquis etiam gentibus communicantes, in unam tecum familiam congregemur* [bless this series of machines that serve to transmit into the waves of the ether so that, communicating the apostolic word even to peoples far away, we will be united with you in one family]." What can we learn from these words? That Pius XI already had in his mind the virtual community, mediated by technology. In fact, while Fascism understood radio as an expansion of gatherings to hear the Duce, Vatican Radio demanded to speak to people's hearts, imagining one unique family. A global medium was thus put at the service of relationships and not propaganda, that is, content. In this blessing, content is finalized by relationships. Today, this is the logic of social networks that, by communicating content, weld relationships. Pius XI, if we think of radio, had a social network in mind, probably because he considered a model of real relationships in this way, rather than as the model of mere radio broadcasting. In this way he had, amongst other things, shown a way by which to understand radio in a sense that is suited to our day.

8. Compendium of the Catechism of the Catholic Church, no. 152, http://www.vatican.va/archive/ENG0015/_INDEX.HTM.

9. Cf. Hobson (2010). In this article, Hobson asks, "What is the emerging church? It is a highly vague movement mainly consisting of ex-Evangelicals, who have found that tradition narrow, inauthentic, illiberal. It is defined by the desire to communicate Christianity to young agnostics—not as Alpha Course fodder, but as fairly trendy, media-savvy, liberal-leftish types who are wary of organised religion. It is above all a presentation style—of openness, of scepticism towards the old fusty dusty forms, of irreverence, of irony, of artiness, of political and environmental engagement. . . . We should reject the assumption that Christian culture takes the form of a stable institution, or even a stable movement. . . . I like the sound of this. I agree that Christian culture must move away from the institutional Church; we must simply dump all that ghastly old baggage of bishops and buildings, rules and power, and start a new sort of Christian cultural presence."

10. See http://www.irs.gov/pub/irs-pdf/p1828.pdf.

11. See http://religionmeetsnewmedia.blogspot.com/2010/08/can -onlinecommunity-be-church-irs-says.html.

12. Compendium of the Catechism of the Catholic Church, no. 147, http://www.vatican.va/archive/ENG0015/_INDEX.HTM.

13. Ibid., nos. 156, 158.

14. For the way in which the Catholic Church is present on the Web, see Vogt (2011). For a valuation in the light of statistics and data, see Arasa, Canton, and Ruiz (2010).

15. See Qureshi (2010). Rima Qureshi is a Pakistani-Canadian and the vice president of Ericsson Response.

16. On the more general theme of religious authority in the era of the Internet, see part II of Højsgaard and Warburg (2005) and Campbell (2007).

17. Catechism of the Catholic Church, no. 890, http://www. vatican.va/archive/ENG0015/_INDEX.HTM.

4. HACKER ETHICS AND CHRISTIAN VISION

1. It is worth highlighting a study on formation for the consecrated life, which might, however, also be useful in understanding how digital communication can be a challenge to more general formation. See Riccieri (2011) and Alday (2011). In regard to formation for the consecrated life, or for that of a priest, it is important to

understand that the objective must not only be the assumption of competences and specific abilities, since "to educate" does not signify "to instruct." The first meaning of "to educate" must be to understand what we are living, that is, to reason through experience and, above all, through our own experience. The first task of a trainer is not to make us attend specific courses on how we can make a blog, or how we can be present on a social network, but to discuss with those being formed how they are living in the digital environment, how they are present on the Web, and with what means, and where there are good and bad experiences, if they have had them. What are their enthusiasms, delusions, temptations, and virtues? Today, seminarians or religious in formation generally already have a presence in the digital world. There is no need to imagine the young as a *tabula rasa* or, worse, as a *tabula da radere*. Asceticism, in this sense, has a value. Sometimes it is good to know when to close connections. However, the objective must not simply be *detachment*, as if the virtual environment were perhaps in itself a temptation, but to learn a mature way of living (both on- and offline, we only have one life!). It is only from evaluation of his own experience that is as mature as possible that it is possible to form an ordained minister or religious who is called to help others to live up to their humanity and spirituality.

2. In http://www.radicalcongruency.com. Among the various personal sites about the emerging Church, see Paul Teusner's Network for New Media, Religion and Digital Culture Studies, http://digitalreligion.tamu.edu/users/paul-emerson-teusner.

3. See Perriman's website at http://www.opensourcetheology.net.

4. See http://www.postost.net/2010/03/brian-mclaren-new-kind-christianitywhat-do-we-do-about-church (page no longer available).

5. See Tapscott and Williams (2008, 289–315) and Anderson (2009), who has a chapter dedicated to synthesizing a sort of "story of free." See also "Religion and Mass Collaboration," https://www.socialtext.net/wikinomics/index.cgi?religion_and_mass_collaboration, and the suggestions on "Faith & Wikinomics—Will Mass Collaboration Change Church?," http://thedigitalsanctuary.org/2007/03/14/faith-wikinomics-will-mass-collaboration-change-church (page no longer available).

6. We understand that, on a commercial level, this poses a problem with rights, since it allows exchange, that is, the sharing of

material protected by copyright, through which sharing, even by those who legally hold rights, becomes a crime. As a result, a movement that holds open source software—and the copyright, or the copyleft, or the author's permission—is emerging. See, for example, the chapter "Dono versus copyright" (Gift versus copyright) in Doronzo (2009, 151–60).

7. See Berra and Meo (2006), in particular the chapter "Dono e cooperazione: un nuovo modello di produzione e di sviluppo" (Gift and cooperation: a new model of production and development), 162–200.

8. See Shirky (2010, 78 and 119) and Benkler (2002). Benkler writes, "Commons-based peer production, the emerging third model of production, I describe here, relies on decentralized information gathering and exchange to reduce the uncertainty of participants. It has particular advantages as an information process for identifying and allocating human creativity available to work on information and cultural resources" (375).

9. See, for example, http://www.mozilla.org/about/governance .html.

5. LITURGY, SACRAMENTS, AND VIRTUAL PRESENCE

1. See http://slangcath.wordpress.com and http://churchoffools .com. See also Jenkins (2008), Kluver and Chen (2008), and Miczek (2008).

2. For more in-depth information, see Jacobs (2007).

3. For the complete text and reactions to it, see http://brownblog. info/?p=886 and http://www.liturgy.co.nz/blog/virtual-eucharist/ 1078.

4. See http://bit.ly/fCAKpB (original site discontinued, but the content is still accessible thanks to Internet Archive).

5. See http://www.twittercommunion.co.uk (site discontinued).

6. See http://homepage.ntlworld.com/tim.ross/twittercommu nion/page6.html (site discontinued).

7. See http://twenty1stcenturychristian.blogspot.com/2010/08/ remote-communion-storm-in-communion-cup.html.

8. See http://lussonline.net.

9. See Denzinger, n. 1747.

10. See http://www.youtube.com/watch?v=Kk8ucBlkMRo.

11. The same publicity strategy is related to the category of magic: "Our most advanced technology in a magical and revolutionary device at an unbelievable price." Note the sketch on the first theological reflections on the topic in http://knightopia.com/blog/2010/02/01/theology-after-google/ and http://youthjusticenetwork.blogspot.com/2010/01/Apples-magical-realism-iPad.html.

12. The consequences of a possible regression in the capacities of abstraction that are tied, for example, to sight are not to be undervalued when we imagine the man of the future. Indirect confirmation is given by something quite positive: it seems that the iPad helps autistic children in their learning processes. Some useful applications for this have already been developed. See http://www.sfweekly.com/2010-08-11/news/ihelp-for-autism.

13. Lévy (1997b, 102) writes: "My angelic bodies in my virtual world express my contribution to collective intelligence or my individual posture with respect to shared knowledge. . . . Within the space that emanates from the collective intelligence, I thus encounter the human other, no longer as flesh and blood, as social rank, an owner of things, but as an angel, an active intelligence—active in himself, but potential for me."

14. This text is available at http://www.nccbuscc.org/liturgy/innews/699.shtml.

15. For a critical discussion on this position, see Herring (2008, 41–43).

16. See Borgmann (2003, 117–28), Borgmann (1992), and Borgmann (1984). For an application of this discourse, see also Gaillardetz (2005).

17. The realism of the graphic interfaces for worship online tends to offer visual elements that are familiar, and thus is of interest. See Hutchings (2010). For reflections that touch on the implications of the aesthetics of virtual places of prayer, see Zijderveld (2010). Also consult the essays in Altemeyer and Bombonatto (2011).

18. See also Meyrowitz (1985) and Soukup (2003, 102–22).

19. Illich's book is about the invention of the scriptures and the fact that reading is not our natural habit, but one of inventions, and all that this carries in the context of digital culture. See also Wolf (2008, 197).

20. See http://www.sharingisgood.org/the-bible-as-augmented-reality.

21. Italian Bishops' Conference, Comunicazione e missione. Direttorio sulle comunicazioni sociali nella missione della Chiesa (Communication and Mission: Directory of Social Communication in the Mission of the Church), no. 43. The entire document is available (in Italian) at http://www.chiesacattolica.it/comunicazione/ucs _2012/attivita/00004047_Direttorio_sulle_comunicazioni_sociali _nella_missione_della_Chiesa.html.

22. See Grillo (2011) and Bonaccorso (2001).

6. THE TECHNOLOGICAL TASKS OF COLLECTIVE INTELLIGENCE

1. Avicenna, in particular, was convinced that while a unique intellect existed as agent, individual intelligence could directly enter into contact with ideas that emanated from God. See Avicenna (2002).

2. In this schema, potential intellect—the pure disposition to receive forms, that is, the content—becomes software, the ensemble of languages and programs. The concrete individual would be the hardware that hosts the software, without its operability being tied to it.

3. See the transcript of a dialogue between Lévy and De Kerckhove, recorded in Florence on March 27, 1998, http://www.media mente.rai.it/home/bibliote/intervis/d/dekerco5.htm.

4. Many have identified Teilhard de Chardin as the precursor of reflections on the Web, and some have begun to reflect on the theological applications of his thinking, taking as their starting points the Jesuit thinker's reflections. See, for example, Cobb (1998).

5. See Schönborn (2007, 141–43). See also Waters (2006, 85–88).

Works Cited

NB: This reference list provides the sources cited by the author in the Italian original. Where available, the English translation of the Italian source is listed instead.

Aime, M. 2002. "Da Mauss al MAUSS." In M. Mauss, *Saggio sul dono. Forma e motivo dello scambio nelle società arcaiche* [A text on the gift. Form and motive of exchange in ancient societies]. Turin: Einaudi.

Aime, M., and A. Cossetta. 2011. *Il dono al tempo di Internet* [The gift in the era of the Internet]. Turin: Einaudi.

Alday, J. M., ed. 2011. *Nuovi media e vita consacrata* [New media and the consecrated life]. Milan: Ancora.

Altemeyer, F., and V. I. Bombonatto. 2011. *Teologia e comunicação. Corpo, palavra e interfaces cibernéticas* [Theology, communication, body, word, and cybernetic interfaces]. São Paulo: Paulinas.

Anderson, C. 2009. *Free: The Future of a Radical Price.* New York: Random House.

Antonelli, P. 2011. *Talk to Me. Design and the Communication between People and Objects.* New York: Moma.

Arasa, D., L. Canton, and L. Ruiz L, eds. 2010. *Religious Internet Communication. Facts, Experiences and Trends in the Catholic Church.* Rome: Edusc.

Avicenna. 2002. *Metafisica. La scienza delle cose divine.* Bompiani, Milano. A parallel English language/Arabic text has been published as *The Metaphysics of the Healing: A Parallel English-Arabic text = al-Shifā': al-Ilahīyāt / Avicenna.* Translated, introduced, and annotated by Michael E. Marmura Provo, UT: Brigham Young University Press, 2005.

Baragli, E., ed. 1973. *Comunicazione, Comunione e Chiesa* [Communication, communion, and church]. Rome: Studio Romano della Comunicazione Sociale.

Baragli, E. 1974. "Mass media e liturgia" [Mass media and liturgy]. In *Comunicazione e pastorale: Sociologia pastorale degli strumenti della comunicazione sociale* [Pastoral Communication: Pastoral Sociology of the Instruments of Social Communication] by Baragali, 195–210. Roma: Studio Romano della Comunicazione Sociale.

Bauman, Z. 2001. *Community: Seeking Safety in an Insecure World.* Cambridge: Polity.

Beaudoin, T. 1998. *Virtual Faith. The Irreverent Spiritual Quest of Generation X.* San Francisco: Jossey-Bass.

Bedell, K. 1999. "Internet Congregations in 1999." http://www.reli gion-research.org/RRAPaper1999.htm.

Benedict XVI. 2009a. "Caritas in veritate." http://www.vatican.va/ holy_father/benedict_xvi/encyclicals/documents/hf_ben-xvi _enc_20090629_caritas-in-veritate_en.html.

———. 2009b. "New Technologies, New Relationships. Promoting a Culture of Respect, Dialogue and Friendship." Message for the 43rd World Day of Social Communications. http://www.vatican .va/holy_father/benedict_xvi/messages/communications/docu ments/hf_ben-xvi_mes_20090124_43rd-world-communications -day_en.html.

———. 2010. "Message of His Holiness Pope Benedict XVI for the 44th World Communications Day." http://www.vatican.va/holy _father/benedict_xvi/messages/communications/documents/hf _ben-xvi_mes_20100124_44th-world-communications-day_en .html.

———. 2011a. "Address of His Holiness Benedict XVI to Participants in the Plenary Assembly of the Pontifical Council for Social Communications." http://www.vatican.va/holy_father/benedict

_xvi/speeches/2011/february/documents/hf_ben-xvi_spe
_20110228_pccs_en.html.

———. 2011b. "Truth, Proclamation and Authenticity of Life in the Digital Age." http://www.vatican.va/holy_father/benedict_xvi/messages/communications/documents/hf_ben-xvi_mes_2011 0124_45th-world-communications-day_en.html.

———. 2012. "Silence and Word: Path of Evangelization." Message of His Holiness for the 46th World Communications Day. May 10. http://www.vatican.va/holy_father/benedict_xvi/messages/communications/documents/hf_ben-xvi_mes_20120124_46th -world-communications-day_en.html.

Benjamin, Walter. 1999. "The Work of Art in the Age of Mechanical Reproduction." In *Illuminations* by Walter Benjamin, 211–44. With an introduction by Hannah Arendt. Translated by Harry Zorn. London/Sydney/Auckland/Parktown: Pimlico Books for Random House.

Benkler, Y. 2002. "Coase's Penguin, or, Linux and the Nature of the Firm." *Yale Law Journal* 112: 371–99.

Berger, D. O. 1996. "Theology in the Brave New World." *Concordia Journal* 22: 195. http://www.csl.edu/resources/publications/concor dia-journal/concordia-journal-archive/.

Berger, P. L., and T. Luckmann. (1967) 2011. *The Social Construction of Reality: A Treatise in the Sociology of Knowledge.* New York: Open Road/Integrated Media.

Berra, M., and A. R. Meo. 2006. *Libertà di software, hardware e cono-scenza. Informatica solidale 2* [Freedom of software, hardware and knowledge. Computer solidarity 2] Milan: Bollati Boringhieri.

Bertani, C. 2007. "Dal brainframe visivo al santo elettronico. In-tervista a Derrick De Kerckhove" [From the visual brainframe to the electronic saint: Interview with Derrick de Kerckhove]. In *Etica del virtuale* [The ethics of the virtual], edited by A. Fabris. Milan: Vita e Pensiero.

Bittanti, M. 2007. Introduzione (Introduction). *Second Life.* By A. Fabris. Rome: Meltemi.

Bonaccorso, G. 2001. "La dimensione comunicativa della liturgia" [The communicative dimension of the liturgy]. In *Teologia e comu-nicazione* [Theology and Communication], edited by G. Giuliodori and G. Lorizio, 129–66. Cinisello Balsamo, Milan: San Paolo.

Bonini, T. 2010. *Così lontano, così vicino. Tattiche mediali per abitare lo spazio* [So far, so near: Media tactics for living in space]. Verona: Ombre Corte.

Borgmann, A. 1984. *Technology and the Character of Contemporary Life. A Philosophical Inquiry.* Chicago: University of Chicago Press.

———. 1992. *Crossing the Postmodern Divide,* Chicago: University of Chicago Press.

———. 1999. *Holding On to Reality. The Nature of Information at the Turn of the Millennium.* Chicago: University of Chicago Press.

———. 2003. *Power Failure: Christianity in the Culture of Technology.* Grand Rapids, MI: Brazos.

Bottazzini, P. 2010. *Googlecrazia. Il mondo in una query* [Googlecrazy: The world in a query]. Milan: Convergenze.

Brasher, B. E. 2004. *Give Me That Online Religion.* New Brunswick, NJ: Rutgers University Press.

Bressan, L. 2010. "Diventare preti nell'era digitale. Risvolti pedagogici e nuovi cammini" [Becoming priests in the digital era: Pedagogical implications and new paths]. *La Rivista del Clero Italiano* XCI: 167–86.

Brewin, K. 2007. *Sign of Emergence. A Vision for Church That Is Organic, Networked, Decentralized, Bottom-Up, Communal, Flexible, Always Evolving.* Grand Rapids, MI: Baker Books.

Brockman, J. 2011. *Is the Internet Changing the Way You Think? The Net's Impact on Our Mind and Future.* New York: Harper Collins.

Bull, M. 2000. *Sounding Out the City: Personal Stereos and the Management of Everyday Life.* Oxford: Berg.

Calvino, I. 1994. *Romanzi e racconti* [Novels and stories]. Vol. 3. Milan: Mondadori.

Campbell, H. 2007. "Who's Got the Power? Religious Authority and the Internet." *Journal of Computer-Mediated Communication* 12. http://jcmc.indiana.edu/vol12/issue3/campbell.html.

Canobbio, G. 2001. "Comunione ecclesiale e comunicazione. La comunicazione in prospettiva ecclesiologica" [Ecclesial communion and communication: Communication from an ecclesiological perspective]. In *Teologia e comunicazione,* edited by G. Giuliodori and G. Lorizio, 167–85. Cinisello Balsamo (MI), Italy: San Paolo.

Carr, N. 2011. *The Shallows: What the Internet Is Doing to Our Brains.* London/New York: W. W. Norton.

Catechism of the Catholic Church. 1993. http://www.vatican.va/ar chive/ENG0015/_INDEX.HTM.

Casey, C. 2006. "Virtual Ritual, Real Faith. The Revirtualization of Religious Ritual in Cyberspace." *Journal of Religions on the Internet* 2: 73–90.

Castells, M. 2003. *The Internet Galaxy: Reflections on the Internet, Business and Society.* Oxford/New York: Oxford University Press.

Cebollada, P., ed. 2005. *Del Génesis a internet. Documentos del Magisterio sobre las comunicaciones sociales* [From Genesis to the Internet: Documents of the magisterium on social communications]. Madrid: Biblioteca de Autores Cristianos.

Cobb, J. J. 1998. *Cybergrace: The Search for God in the Digital World.* New York: Crown.

Coffy, R. 1968. *Teilhard de Chardin e il socialismo* [Teilhard de Chardin and Socialism]. Alba, Italy: Edizioni Paoline.

Collins-Mayo, S., B. Mayo, S. Nash, and C. Cocksworth. 2010. *The Faith of Generation Y.* London: Church House Publishing,

Conferenza Episcopale Italiana (CEI). 2010. *Educare alla vita buona del Vangelo. Orientamenti pastorali dell'Episcopato italiano per il decennio 2010–2020.* http://www.chiesacattolica.it/documenti/ 2010/10/00015206_educare_alla_vita_buona_del_vangelo_orien .html.

Davis, E. 1995. "Technopagans. May the Astral Plane Be Reborn in Cyberspace." *Wired* (July). http://www.wired.com/wired/archive/ 3.07/technopagans.html.

———. 1999. *TechGnosis: Myth, Magic, and Mysticism in the Age of Information.* New York: Three Rivers Press.

De Biase, L. 2003. *eDeologia. Critica del fondamentalismo digitale* (eDeology: Critique of digital fundamentalism). Roma/Bari: Laterza.

De Carli, L. 1997. *Internet. Memoria e Oblio* [Internet: Memory and Oblivion]. Torino: Bollati Boringhieri.

Dini, A. 2005. "La matematica delle cuffie che 'sottraggono' il rumore" [The mathematics of the headphones that "take away" the noise]. *Nòva*, supplement to *Il Sole 24 Ore*, October 20.

Doronzo R. 2009. *Chiesa e mezzi di comunicazione: un rapporto da approfondire* [Church and the means of communication: A relationship to deepen]. Bari: Ed Insieme.

Dulles, A. 1971. "The Church Is Communications." *Catholic Mind* (October): 5.

———. 1987. *Models of the Church*. Garden City, NY: Image Books.

Eilers, F.-J., and R. Giannatelli, eds. 1996. *Chiesa e comunicazione sociale: documenti fondamentali* [Church and social communication: The fundamental documents]. Torino: ElleDiCi, Leumann.

Ellul, J. 2009. *Il sistema tecnico: La gabbia delle società contemporanee* [The Technical System: Contemporary Society's Cage]. Milan: Jaca, Book.

Estes, D. 2009. *SimChurch: Being the Church in the Virtual World*. Grand Rapids, Milan: Zonverdan.

Fallon, P. K. 2009. *The Metaphysics of Media: Toward an End of Postmodern Cynicism and the Construction of a Virtuous Reality*. Scranton, PA: University of Scranton Press.

Felton, D. A. 1989. "The Unavoidable Dialogue: Five Interfaces between Theology and Communication." *Media Development* 36: 17–23.

Ferraris, M. 2005. *Dove sei? Ontologia del telefonino* [Where are you? The ontology of the cell phone]. Milan: Bompiani.

———. 2011. *Anima e iPad* [Soul and iPad]. Parma: Guanda.

Ferri, P. 2011. *Nativi digitali* [Digital natives]. Milan: Bruno Mondadori.

Foley, E. 2005. "Theological Reflection, Theology and Technology: When Baby Boomer Theologians Teach Generations X and Y." *Theological Education* 41: 45–56.

Formenti, C. 2008. *Incantati dalla rete. Immaginari, utopie e conflitti nell'epoca di internet* [Enchanted by the web: Imagineries, utopias and conflicts in the era of the Internet]. Milan: Raffaello Cortina.

Forte, B. 2006. "To save, to convert, to justify. I linguaggi della rete e la nostalgia di trascendenza" [To save, to convert, to justify: the languages of the Web and the nostalgia for transcendence]. Presentation at XLIV Congress of the Italian Society of Psychiatry, October 30. http://bit.ly/9MD76s.

Friesen, D. J. 2009. *Thy Kingdom Connected. What the Church Can Learn From Facebook, the Internet, and Other Networks*. Grand Rapids, MI: Baker Books.

Fuller, M. 1995. *Atoms and Icons. Discussion of the Relationships between Science and Theology*. London: Mowbray.

————. 2010. "Science and theology: Consonances." *Thinking Faith*, November 5. http://www.thinkingfaith.org/articles/20101105_1 .htm.

Gagliardi, A. 2002. *Tommaso d'Aquino e Averroè. La visione di Dio* [Thomas Aquinas and Averroes: The Vision of God]. Rubbettino, Italy (CZ): Soveria Mannelli.

Gaillardetz, R. R. 2005. *Transforming Our Days: Spirituality, Community, and Liturgy in a Technological Culture*, New York: Crossroad.

Gardner, H. 1983. *Frames of Mind: The Theories of Multiple Intelligences.* New York: Basic Books.

————. 2006. *Five Minds for the Future.* Boston, MA: Harvard Business School Press.

————. 2010. *Formae mentis. Saggio sulla pluralità dell'intelligenza* [Formae mentis: A text on the plurality of understanding]. Milan: Feltrinelli.

————. 2011. *Cinque chiavi per il futuro* [Five keys for the future]. Milan: Feltrinelli.

George, S. 2006. *Religion and Technology in the 21st Century. Faith in the World.* Hershey, PA: Information Science Publishing.

Giaccardi, C., ed. 2010a. *Abitanti della rete. Giovani, relazioni e affetti nell'epoca digitale* [Inhabitants of the Web: The young, relationships and affections in the digital era]. Milan, Italy: Vita e Pensiero.

————. 2010b. "Liturgie di presenza. 'Canali magici' e vita quotidiana" [Liturgy of the Presence: "Magic Channels" and everyday life]. *Comunicazioni sociali* 3: 247–59.

Gibson, William. 1984. *Neuromancer.* New York: Ace Publishing.

Giuliodori, G., and G. Lorizio, eds. 2001. *Teologia e comunicazione* [Theology and Communication]. San Paolo (MI), Italy: Cinisello Balsamo.

Granieri, G. 2009. *Umanità accresciuta. Come la tecnologia ci sta cambiando* [Increased humanity: How technology is changing us]. Rome/Bari: Laterza.

Grillo, A. 2011. "Segni, riti e atto di fede nel cyberspazio: internet come 'atto second' e come atto primo" [Signs, rites, and act of faith in cyberspace: Internet as the "second act" and as the "first act"]. *Credere oggi* XXX 3: 29–43.

Grotti, A. 2010. *ComunIcare. Prendersi cura nel tempo della rivoluzione digitale* [To Communicate: Taking care of oneself in the era of the digital revolution]. Rome: Ave.

Halavais, A. 2009. *Search Engine Society*. Cambridge: Polity Press.

Hawthorne, N. 2009. *The House of the Seven Gables*. Rockville, MD: Arc Manor LLC.

Heim, M. 1991. "The Erotic Ontology of Cyberspace." In *Cyberspace: First Steps*, edited by M. Benedikt, 58–80. Cambridge, MA: MIT Press.

———. 1998. *Virtual Realism*, Oxford: Oxford University Press.

Herring, D. 2005. "Virtual as Contextual. A Net News Theology." In *Religion and Cyberspace*, edited by M. T. Højsgaard and M. Warburg, 149–65. New York: Routledge.

———. 2008. "Towards Sacrament in Cyberspace." *Epworth Review* 35: 41–45.

Highland, M., and G. Yu. 2008. "Communicating Spiritual Experience with Video Game Technology." *Heidelberg Journal of Religions on the Internet* 3: 267–89.

Himanen, Pekka. 2001. *The Hacker Ethic and the Spirit of the Information Age*. London, Sydney, Auckland, Parktown: Secker and Warburg.

Hobson, T. 2010. "A New Model Christianity." http://www.guardian.co.uk/commentisfree/belief/2010/jul/07/religion-christianity-emergingevangelical.

Højsgaard, M. T. 2005. "Cyber-religion: On the Cutting Edge between the Virtual and the Real." In *Religion and Cyberspace*, edited by M. T. Højsgaard and M. Warburg, 50–63. New York: Routledge.

Højsgaard, M. T., and M. Warburg, eds. 2005. *Religion and Cyberspace*. New York: Routledge.

Howe, N., and W. Strauss. 2000. *Millennials Rising. The Next Great Generation*. New York: Vintage Books.

Hutchings, T. 2010. "The Politics of Familiarity: Visual, Liturgical and Organizational Conformity in the Online Church. *Heidelberg Journal of Religions on the Internet* 4: 63–86.

Illich, I. 1993. *In the Vineyard of the Text: A Commentary to Hugh's Didascalicon*. Translated by Valentina Borremans. Chicago/London: University of Chicago Press.

Illuminate, A. 1996. *Averroè e l'intelletto pubblico. Antologia di scritti di Ibn Rushd sull'anima* [Averroes and the public intellect. An anthology of the writings of Ibn Rushd on the Soul]. Rome: Manifesto libri.

————. 2003. *Del comune. Cronache del General Intellect* [The Commune: Chronicles of the General Intellect]. Rome: Manifesto libri.

Jacobs, S. 2007. "Virtually Sacred: The Performance of Asynchronous Cyber-rituals in Online Spaces." *Journal of Computer-Mediated Communication* 12, no.3. http://jcmc.indiana.edu/vol12/issue3/jacobs .html.

Jenkins, S. 2008. "Rituals and Pixels. Experiments in Online Church." *Heidelberg Journal of Religions on the Internet* 3: 95–115.

John Paul II. 1985. "Social Communications for a Christian Promotion of Youth." Message for the 19th World Day of Social Communication. http://www.vatican.va/holy_father/john_paul_ii/ messages/communications/documents/hf_jp-ii_mes_15041985 _world-communications-day_en.html

————. 1989. "Religion in the Mass Media." Message for the 23rd World Day of Communication. http://www.vatican.va/holy_father/ john_paul_ii/messages/communications/documents/hf_jp-ii_ mes_24011989_world-communications-day_en.html.

————. 2005. "Apostolic Letter: The Rapid Development of the Holy Father." http://www.vatican.va/holy_father/john_paul_ii/apost _letters/documents/hf_jp-ii_apl_20050124_il-rapido-sviluppo_en .html.

Kluver R., and Y. Chen. 2008. "The Church of Fools: Virtual Ritual and Material Faith." *Heidelberg Journal of Religions on the Internet* 3: 116–43.

Koczon, C. 2011. "Orbital Content." *A List Apart*, no. 326. April 19. http://alistapart.com/article/orbital-content.

Lellouche, R. 1997. "Théorie de l'écran" [Theory of the screen]. *Traverse* 2 (April). http://www2.centrepompidou.fr/traverses/numero2/ textes/lellouche.html.

Leone, M. 2010. "Varietà virtuali dell'esperienza religiosa. Uno studio sulla natura umana in Second Life." [Virtual varieties of religious experience: A study of human nature in Second Life]. *Humanitas* LXV, 5–6: 791–809.

Levinson, P. 2003. *Realspace. The Fate of Physical Presence in the Digital Age, On and Off Planet.* London/New York: Routledge.

Lévy, P. 1997a. *Becoming Virtual: Reality in the Digital Age.* Translated by Robert Bononno. London/New York: Plenum Trade.

———. 1997b. *Collective Intelligence: Mankind's Emerging World in Cyberspace*. Translated by Robert Bononno. New York and London: Plenum.

———. 2001. *Cyberculture*. Vol. 4 in the Electronic Mediations Series. Translated by R. Bononno. Minneapolis/London: University of Minnesota Press.

Levy, S. 2010. *Hackers: Heroes of the Computer Revolution–25th Anniversary Edition*. Sebastopol, CA: O'Reilly Media.

Lih, A. 2009. *The Wikipedia Revolution: How a Bunch of Nobodies Created the World's Greatest Encyclopedia*. London: Aurum.

Livingstone, Sonia, and L. Haddon, eds. 2009. *Kids Online: Opportunities and Risks for Children*. Bristol: Policy Press.

Lövheim, M., and A. G. Linderman. 2005. "Constructing Religious Identity on the Internet." In *Religion and Cyberspace*, edited by M. T. Højsgaard and M. Warburg, 121–37. New York: Routledge.

Lynch, J. 2011. *Il profumo dei limoni. Tecnologia e rapporti umani nell'era di Facebook*, Turin: Lindau. *The Scent of Lemons: Technology and Relationships in the Age of Facebook* (London: Darton, Longman, Todd, 2012).

Mancini, R. 2011. *La logica del dono. Meditazioni sulla società che credeva d'essere un mercato* [The logic of the gift: Meditations on the society that believed it was a market]. Padova: Messaggero.

Manovich, L. 2010. *Software culturale*. Milan, Italy: Olivares.

Mayer-Schönberger, V. 2010. *Delete. Il diritto all'oblio nell'era digitale* [Delete: The right to oblivion in the digital era]. Milan, Italy: Egea.

McLuhan, M. 1999. The *Medium and the Light*. Edited by E. McLuhan and J. Szkiarek. Toronto: Stoddart.

———. (1964) 2004. *Understanding Media: The Extensions of Man*. London/New York: Routledge.

Meyrowitz, J. 1985. *No Sense of Place. The Impact of Electronic Media on Social Behavior*. New York: Oxford University Press.

Miczek, N. 2008. Online Rituals in Virtual Worlds. Christian Online Service between Dynamics and Stability." *Heidelberg Journal of Religions on the Internet* 3: 144–73.

Mitchell, N. 2005. "Il rituale e i nuovi media" [Ritual and the new media]. *Concilium* XLI: 118.

Monsma, S. M., ed. 1986. *Responsible Technology. A Christian Perspective*. Grand Rapids, MI: Eerdmans.

Müller, Gerhard Ludwig. 2010. "Nella Rete con gli occhi aperti [On the web with open eyes]." Paper delivered at the Plenary Assembly of the Pontifical Council for Culture, November 13, 2010. http://www.vatican.va/news_services/or/or.quo/cultura/2010/262 q04a1.html

Mumford, L. (1934) 1963. *Technics and Civilization*. Chicago: University of Chicago Press.

Musso, P. 2007. *L'ideologia delle reti* [The Ideology of the Network]. Milano: Apogeo.

Oldenburg, R. 1989. *The Great Good Place: Cafes, Coffee Shops, Community Centers, Beauty Parlors, General Stores, Bars, Hangouts, and How They Get You Through the Day*. New York: Paragon House.

O'Leary, S. D. 2005. "Utopian and dystopian possibilities of networked religion in the new millennium." In *Religion and Cyberspace*, edited by M. T. Højsgaard–M. Warburg, 38–49. New York: Routledge.

Ong, W. J. 1967. *The Presence of the Word. Some Prolegomena for Cultural and Religious History*. New Haven, CT: Yale University Press.

———. 1969. "Communication Media and the State of Theology." *Cross Currents* 19: 462–80.

Ottmar, J. 2005. "Cyberetica: nuove sfide o vecchi problemi?" [Cyberethics: New challenges or old problems?]. *Concilium* XLI: 20–35.

Pace, E., and G. Giordan. 2010. "La religione come comunicazione nell'era digitale" [Religion as communication in the digital era] *Humanitas* LXV, 5–6: 761–81. http://www.morcelliana.it/ita/MENU/Le_Riviste/Humanitas/or?uid=morcelliana.main.index&oid=53634.

Pariser, E. 2011. *The Filter Bubble: What the Internet Is Hiding from You*. New York: Penguin Press.

Paul VI. 1964. "Lumen Gentium." November 21.

Perkin, H. 1970. *The Age of the Railway*. London: Panther.

Pittman, Tom. 2008. "The God of Truth: Reforming the Feminized American Church." http://www.ittybittycomputers.com/Truth/GodOfTruth.htm.

Pompili, D. 2010. "L'eredità di 'Testimoni digitali'" [The inheritance of "Digital Witnesses"]. Contribution of the director of the National Office for Social Communication of the Italian Bishops' Conference at the conference "Dioceses on the Web," November 23. http://www.diocesinrete.it.

———. 2011. *Il nuovo nell'antico. Comunicazione e testimonianza nell'era digitale* [The new in the old: Communication and witnessing in the digital era]. Cinisello Balsamo (MI), Italy: San Paolo.

Proserpio, L. 2011. *Comportamenti digitali. Essere giovani ed essere vecchi ai tempi di Internet* [Digital behaviors: To be young and to be old in the era of the Internet]. Milan, Italy: Egea.

Qureshi, Rima. 2010. "Per chiedere aiuto serve una voce. Lei lo sa. E per rompere il silenzio usa la rete" (To call for help, you need a voice. You know it. To break the silence, use the web). Wired.it, October 11. http://mag.wired.it/news/storie/internet-for-peace-rima -qureshi.html.

Queau, P. 1989. *Metaxu: Théorie de l'art intermédiaire* [Metaxu: Theories of intermediary art]. Seyssel: Champ Vallon.

Rahner, H. 1971. *L'ecclesiologia dei Padri. Simboli della Chiesa.* [The Ecclesiology of the Fathers: Symbols of the Church]. Rome: Edizioni Paoline.

Rahner, K. 1978. *Foundations of Christian Faith: An Introduction to the Idea of Christianity.* Translated by William V. Dych. London: Darton, Longman and Todd.

Raymond, E. S. 2001. "How to Become a Hacker." http://www.catb .org/esr/faqs/hacker-howto.html.

———. 2010. "La cattedrale e il bazar" [The cathedral and the bazaar]. In *Etica e responsabilità sociale delle tecnologie dell'informazione, vol. 1: Valori e deontologia professionale* [Ethics and social responsibility of information technologies, Vol. 1: Values and professional deontology], edited by S. Di Guardo, P. Maggiolini, and N. Patrignani, 131–55. Milan, Italy: Franco Angeli.

Riccieri, P. 2011. *Formazione a portata di click. Comunicazione digitale e santificazione della mente* [Formation at a click: Digital communication and the sanctification of the mind]. Milan: Edizioni Paoline.

Rice, J. 2009. *The Church of Facebook. How the Hyperconnected Are Redefining Community.* Colorado Springs, CO: David Cook.

Robinson-Neal, A. 2008. "Enhancing the Spiritual Relationship: The Impact of Virtual Worship on the Real World Church Experience." *Heidelberg Journal of Religions on the Internet* 3: 228–45.

Roblimo. 2002. "Larry Wall On Perl, Religion, and . . ." http:// interviews.slashdot.org/story/02/09/06/1343222/Larry-Wall-On -Perl-Religion.

Roof, W. C. 1999. *Spiritual Marketplace: Baby Boomers and the Remaking of American Religion.* Princeton, NJ: Princeton University Press.

Rosen, J. 2010. "Il web non dimentica mai" [The web never forgets]. *Internazionale* September, 17–23, 43.

Sanavio, M. 2011. "I cambiamenti antropologici dell'era elettronica" [Anthropological changes in the electronic era]. *Credere oggi* XXX, no. 3: 7–17.

Schirrmacher, F. 2010. *La libertà ritrovata. Come (continuare a) pensare nell'era digitale* [Liberty refound. How to (continue to) think in the digital age]. Torino: Codice.

Schönborn, C. 2007. *Chance or Purpose? Creation, Evolution and a Rational Faith.* San Francisco: Ignatius Press.

Schroeder, R., N. Heather, and R. M. Lee. 1998. "The Sacred and the Virtual: Religion in Multi-User Virtual Reality. *Journal of Computer-Mediated Communication* 4, no. 2 (December). http://jcmc.indiana.edu/vol4/issue2/schroeder.html

Sequeri, P. 2001. "Comunicazione, fede e cultura" [Communication, faith and culture]. In *Teologia e comunicazione* [Theology and Communication], edited by G. Giuliodori and G. Lorizio, 11–28. San Paolo (MI), Italy: Cinisello Balsamo.

———. 2010. *Charles de Foucauld. Il Vangelo viene da Nazaret* [Charles de Foucauld: the Gospel comes from Nazareth]. Milan, Italy: Vita e Pensiero.

Shirky, C. 2009. *Here Comes Everybody: How Change Happens when People Come Together.* Penguin Books.

———. 2010. *Cognitive Surplus: Creativity and Generosity in a Connected Age.* New York and London: Penguin Press.

Sofri, L. 2005. "Il 'life is random' della Apple non è poi così random" [Apple's "Life is random" is not, then, so random]. *Il Foglio*, January 14. www.ilfoglio.it.

Soukup, P. 1983. *Communication and Theology. Introduction and Review of the Literature.* London: World Association for Christian Communication.

———. 2002. "The Context, Structure, and Content of Theology from a Communication Perspective." *Gregorianum* 83, no. 1: 131–43.

———. 2003. "The Structure of Communication as a Challenge for Theology." *Teología y Vida* XLIV: 102–22.

———. 2006. "Recent Work in Communication and Theology: A Guide for the CICS." In *Cross Connections. Interdisciplinary*

Communications Studies at the Gregorian University, edited by Jacob Srampickal, Giuseppe Mazza, and Lloyd Baugh, 121–46. Rome: Università Gregoriana.

Soukup, P. A., F. J. Buckley, and D. C. Robinson. 2001. "The Influence of Information Technologies on Theology." *Theological Studies* 62: 366–77.

Spadaro, A. 2001. "Dio nella Rete. Forme del religioso in internet" [God on the Web: Forms of the religious on the Internet]. *La Civiltà Cattolica* III: 15–27.

———. 2006. *Connessioni. Nuove forme della cultura al tempo di internet*, [Connections. New forms of culture in the era of the Internet]. Bologna, Italy: Pardes.

———. 2007. "Second Life: il desiderio di un' 'altra vita'" [Second Life: The desire for an "other life"]. *La Civiltà Cattolica* III: 266–78.

———. 2010a. "La 'magia' dell'iPad sarà la morte del web?" [The "magic" of the iPad, will it be the death of the Web?]. *La Civiltà Cattolica* IV: 19–32.

———. 2010b. *Web 2.0. Reti di relazione* [Web 2.0: Webs of relationship]. Milan, Italy: Edizioni Paoline.

Tapscott, D., and A. D. Williams. 2008. *Wikinomics: How Mass Collaboration Changes Everything.* London: Atlantic Books.

Teilhard de Chardin, P. 1969. *The Future of Man.* Translated by Norman Denny. London and New York: Fontana Books.

———. 1970. *The Activation of Energy.* Translated by René Hague. London: Collins.

———. 1971. *Human Energy.* Translated by J. M. Cohen. New York: A Helen and Kurt Wolff Book for Harcourt Brace Jovanovich. http://ia700607.us.archive.org/23/items/HumanEnergy/Human_Energy_text.pdf.

———. 2004. *Le Milieu Divin: An Essay on the Interior Life.* London/New York: Fontana Books.

———. 2008. *The Phenomenon of Man.* London: HarperCollins.

Teusner, P. 2008. "Religion 2.0. Heralding a new wave of online religion." http://rmit.academia.edu/PaulEmerson/Papers.

Thomas, A. 2011. *Digital Disciple. Real Christianity in a Virtual World.* Nashville, TN: Abingdon Press.

Tilliette. X. 2008. *Eucarestia e filosofia* [Eucharist and philosophy]. Brescia, Italy: Morcelliana.

Tremolada, L. 2009. "Riforma mentis [Reforming the mind]." *Nòva*, supplement to *Il Sole 24 Ore*, March 14.

Turkle, S, ed. 2008. *The Inner History of Devices*. Cambridge, MA: MIT Press.

————. 2011. *Alone Together. Why We Expect More from Technology and Less from Each Other*. New York: Basic Books.

Vecchi, E. 2010. *Antenna Crucis: Il passaggio dall'analogico al digitale* [Antenna Crucis: The journey from the analog to the digital]. Bologna: EDB.

Vogt, B. 2011. *The Church and New Media: Blogging Converts, On-line Activists, and Bishops Who Tweet*. Huntington, IN: Our Sunday Visitor.

Waters, B. 2006. *From Human to Posthuman. Christian Theology and Technology in a Postmodern World*. Aldershot, UK: Ashgate.

Watson, R. 2011. *Future Minds: How the Digital Age Is Changing Our Minds, Why This Matters, and What We Can Do About It*. London and Boston, MA: Nicholas Brealey.

Weber, Max. 2002. *The Protestant Ethic and the Spirit of Capitalism and Other Writings*. Translated by Peter R. Baehr and Gordon C. Wells. New York: Penguin.

Whitsitt, L. 2011. *Open Source Church. Making Room for the Wisdom of All*. Herndon, VA: Alban.

Wolf, M. 2008. *Proust and the Squid: The Story and Science of the Reading Brain*. New York: HarperCollins.

Zijderveld, T. 2010. "The Transformation of the Prayer Wall." *Heidelberg Journal of Religions on the Internet* 4: 131–47.

Zoja, L. 2009. *La morte del prossimo* [The death of the neighbor]. Turin: Einaudi.

Index